The Psychology of Price

The Psychology of Price

How to use price to increase demand, profit and customer satisfaction

Leigh Caldwell

crimson

The Psychology of Price: How to use price to increase demand, profit and customers satisfaction

Published in Great Britain in 2012 by
Crimson Publishing Ltd
Westminster House
Kew Road
Richmond
Surrey
TW9 2ND

Author: Leigh Caidwell

British Library Cataloguing in Publication Data
A catalogue record for this book is available from the British Library.

ISBN 978 1 78059 007 3

Typeset by IDSUK (DataConnection) Ltd
Printed and bound in the UK by Ashford Colour Press, Gosport, Hants

Contents

Acknowledgements   vii

Introduction   ix

The seven principles of pricing   xiii

Chapter 1 Pricing as positioning   1

Chapter 2 Cost-based calculations   16
    In focus: Famous prices in history   23

Chapter 3 Reading the customer's mind   27
    Case study: Cereals at Tesco   32
    Case study: Jewellery maker   34

Chapter 4 Segmentation   41
    In focus: Does 99p pricing work?   47

Chapter 5 New launches, belief and fairness   49
    Case study: A specialist consultancy and its reseller   52

Chapter 6 Memory and expectations, trials and reframing your prices   56
    In focus: Should you increase your prices in line with inflation?   62

Chapter 7 Anchoring   65
    Case study: Business consultancy   68

Chapter 8 Competition   76
    In focus: Pricing publicity   88

Chapter 9 Decoys   91
    Case study: Decoys on services   93
    Case study: Self-decoying   99

Chapter 10 Paying tomorrow for what you get today   102
    In focus: Negotiating   109

Chapter 11 The tea party 112

Chapter 12 Bundling 120
    In focus: Name your own price 128

Chapter 13 Free offers 130

Chapter 14 Upselling 138
    In focus: Occasional versus frequent purchases 147

Chapter 15 Absorption and value pricing 150
    Case study: Software company 154
    Case study: Marketing consultant 157

Chapter 16 Other people's money 162
    In focus: Should you publish your prices? 168

Chapter 17 Managing the pricing environment 170

Chapter 18 The psychology of giving 179
    In focus: How many pricing models are there? 188

Chapter 19 The ethics and law of pricing 191

Epilogue 196

Bibliography and further reading 205

Appendix A. A pricing diagnostic 218
    30 questions to ask to find out if your
    pricing is optimal 218
    A quick-reference method for pricing
    a new product 221

Appendix B. A theory of psychology
and cognition: the background to this book 223

Index 229

Acknowledgements

As a teenager, I had a bet with my brother that I'd write a book and have it published by the time I reached the age of ... well, let's just say I missed the deadline. But thanks, Owen, for helping provide the initial, indirect stimulus for this work.

The rest of my family have also provided love and support over the years and I'd never have been in the position to write this without the framework and happiness that they provided. My deep gratitude to all of you.

The idea to write this particular book arose from many conversations, long walks and glasses of wine over the years with Annette, who has inspired many ideas and achievements by me and other people. More encouragement and thoughts came from Ebru and from Emma, whose introduction to Ali Yates at Crimson initiated the final part of the process.

The content of the book is informed by many years of doing business, and everyone I've worked with has taught me something. So if we've worked together over the years then you have influenced this book. Special thanks to Bastiaan, Daniel, David, Nabil, Philip, Rajiv and Safina for many conversations and collaborations that helped shape my understanding of this field. Helder Miguel also helped nudge me onto this path.

During the writing process both my productivity and sustenance were aided by the hospitality of Shani Hiraoka in Honolulu and everyone at Pret A Manger in Stamford Street.

More direct input came from Sally Holloway via Tim Harford, from the folks at the Society of Authors, from my editor Ian Wallis and from those who kindly read early drafts. Thaddaeus Frogley went well beyond the call of duty, giving extensive and detailed comments on the entire manuscript, as did Kay Caldwell, Alice Moseley, Phil Lord and Martin Caldwell. My good friends John, Paul and George led by example, giving me their books to review before I wrote mine; any authors named Ringo are invited to email me to complete the set.

Introduction

About half of the contents of this book were originally offered as a training manual for partners and directors of major companies, alongside an expert consulting and research service, at £155 – a bargain considering it could increase your income by hundreds of thousands of pounds each year.

We slashed the price to just £33.50 as a promotional offer, and had a surge of interest from smaller companies.

And now it's been published in paperback so we can get the message out to as many people as possible. The new low price: an irresistible £14.99.

See what I did there? In theory, the previous price of this book should be irrelevant to today's reader. In reality, it's not. The psychological power of naming a higher price implicitly makes people believe that a product has a higher value.

For years, setting prices in the businesses I was involved in, I wondered about the psychology of my customers. Like most new business owners I started out by setting a price based on my costs plus a margin. Sometimes the clients would negotiate and sometimes we'd have to match the price of a competitor. The whole time, though, I was convinced that I must be missing something that was going on inside the heads of my customers. If selling a DVD at £9.99 really works better than selling it at £10, surely there must be something I could use in my pricing strategy too.

In 2002 Daniel Kahneman won the Nobel Prize for Economics. This was when the science of behavioural economics, which combines the practice of economics with the experimental discoveries of psychology, started to become more widely known. As I started learning about it, I soon found that this new research had the answers I'd been looking for. It reveals how consumers perceive different price points, whether it is better to negotiate down from a high starting price, whether people will pay more for a monthly contract, and how to persuade clients to pay for the value they are getting. Eventually I set up a business which specialises in providing pricing advice – the advice that is encapsulated in this book.

Behavioural economics research has revealed a rich set of discoveries relating to how people buy products and services, and how much they are willing to pay. From this research, we and other pricing specialists have designed at least 20 different new pricing approaches, including insights into setting basic positioning, segmentation and pricing strategy, how to present prices in retail or business-to-business environments, and how to use pricing to ensure loyalty without giving up profit margins.

It turns out that psychology is one of the main influences on successful pricing. For some products and services, like those of a London-based software company we worked with, the right psychological approach can increase revenues by more than 200%. The difference isn't always that great: we worked with a magazine publisher in a declining market and the improvement was more like 10%. In every case, understanding consumer psychology gives you the ability to improve your pricing power and increase your profits. Indeed, a business must get its approach to pricing right in order to survive and grow; it is a fundamental matter of strategy, not an optional extra.

This is the first book to tell you, step by step, how to use the psychology of price in your business; no matter what you sell, whether a product or a service, to consumers, to other businesses, or to government. It starts with the first steps in using price to position your product or service, then explains how to price differently for different segments of your market, followed by a series of pricing techniques that help you work with, rather than against, the way your customers' minds work.

Along the way you'll read the story of a unique business: the Chocolate Teapot Company. This is a company which used pricing strategies to create a whole new product category, achieve a premium position for it in several markets, and make big profits by understanding the psychology of its customers. It's also a fictional company, so don't expect to see chocolate teapots on the shelves of your local supermarket any time soon — but everything that happens in this book is based on real examples from other businesses.

Each chapter is divided into three sections.

The first part of each chapter tells the story of the Chocolate Teapot Company, showing a new example of how its founders used pricing techniques to launch a product, increase profits, widen its customer base or defend against competitors. The second part explains the particular pricing approach in more detail, discusses the psychological reasons behind it, and provides other case studies of businesses which have used this approach. The third part is a 'How to apply it' toolkit, giving a step-by-step methodology for applying this technique in your business.

At the end of the book is a list of sources where you can find out more about the research and theories that this book is based on, including references to books and articles where you can learn more.

You can read through the book from start to finish. Or you may prefer to focus just on the story, the discussions or the toolkit: each part can stand alone, though if you read them together each one will help to illuminate the others.

Every business is different, and you will find that some of the techniques and chapters are more relevant to your company than others. In any case, they will all give you some insight into how people think, and how that translates into what they buy.

You can also find the supporting materials and electronic versions of most parts of the toolkit on the book's website, www.psyprice.com.

Please do visit the site, talk to other readers and send me your thoughts. I'd particularly enjoy seeing examples of clever pricing approaches you've used in your own business. The best examples will be promoted on the site and, with your permission, may be used as case studies in future editions of this book.

The seven principles of pricing

1. Pricing should be based on the value to the customer, not the cost to you.

2. Prices should be tangible, so your customers can see what they get for what they pay.

3. Prices should be comparable – on terms that you control.

4. If you want to change your prices, you must reframe the service or product.

5. Price differentiation is the key enabler of profit.

6. Pricing communication shapes the client's perception of value.

7. You must be prepared to lose some sales in order to increase profits.

Chapter 1
Pricing as positioning

I burst out laughing when she told me the name of the product.

"Chocolate teapots? You're joking, right?"

Maggie smiled. "Not at all. But I'm glad you reacted that way. I think we're going to get a lot of attention with this."

She opened a cardboard packet and carefully removed an object about the size of a grapefruit. It did, indeed, appear to be shaped like a teapot – and made of a substance which looked just like milk chocolate.

A kettle was just coming to the boil. She opened the lid of the teapot, placed some leaves inside and, to my puzzlement, poured the boiling water straight in. Somehow it wasn't melting.

She handed the teapot to me and I realised that the object itself was made of a thin shell of clear plastic. The brown, in fact, was fading as the chocolate layer inside started to melt.

"You can pour now or wait longer if you'd like it a bit sweeter. Try it," she said, handing me a cup.

I poured out a small amount. It tasted remarkable. The softly aromatic tea flavour was balanced by a light note of sweetness, creaminess and bitter cocoa. I sipped it for a few moments then tried pouring out a little more. This time it was stronger, with the tea and chocolate competing for dominance – maybe a little too sweet and intense for my taste. By now the chocolate had all dissolved. After a minute more, I poured out the last of it and the tea had strengthened, dominating the flavours now with just a relatively soft note of cream and sweetness balancing it.

"What a strange experience," I said. "Might take some getting used to, but I think you've invented something . . . quite good."

Maggie smiled. "Nobody really knows what to make of it at first. But mostly people like it – if they take sugar in their tea. I'm developing a bitter version for those who don't."

Maggie, whom I'd known since first seeing her pricing methods used in a shop a few years ago had invited me to visit her new company and write something about it. I wasn't sure yet what the story was going to be, though it was immediately obvious that the product was original enough to be worth writing up. When I first met her, she was working in photography so I wondered if her product might be something related to mobile phones or technology. I had not expected a cup of tea.

"Anyway," she went on, "the flavour isn't what I want to show you. The really interesting part is this."

She opened a door and invited me through to a new room laid out a bit like a shop, with a series of different display shelves.

"Before I show this to you," she asked me, "how much do you think you would pay for one of those teapots?"

I thought about it. "It's very hard to say. I've never really seen anything like it before. How much does it cost to make?"

"Well, there's an interesting question," she said. "But I'm not going to answer it. Have a look at this."

She pointed me towards the first set of shelves. It was laid out like a supermarket aisle, with jars of instant coffee, bags of filter coffee, boxes of 80 and 160 teabags, and, next to them, the chocolate teapots. I looked more closely, to see the prices.

100g Nescafé Instant	*£2.49*
100g Gold Blend	*£3.39*

80 Tetley teabags	*£1.79*
250g Lavazza coffee	*£3.29*
Pack of six chocolate teapots	*£2.79*
Pack of 12 chocolate teapots	*£4.95*

"I'm not sure I'd buy them very often at that price," I said. "I only get six cups for the same price as a whole jar of coffee. It doesn't seem like good value. Are people willing to pay that much for it?"

"Well done – you've spotted the flaw in the positioning here," she replied. "So let me show you this instead."

The next set of shelves looked more like the display in an Italian café. Cups of various sizes were laid out with price tags beside them:

Cappuccino – small	*£1.89*
Cappuccino – medium	*£2.29*
Cappuccino – large	*£2.59*
Americano – small	*£1.69*
Americano – medium	*£2.05*
Americano – large	*£2.35*
Espresso	*£1.29*
Double espresso	*£1.79*
Vanilla frappuccino	*£3.49*
Chocolate teapot	*£2.89*

"OK, I can see how people would buy that," I said. "It's pretty much in the same range as everything else. I can imagine buying it at that price."

"Well, let's look at one more before you decide."

The final shelving unit was actually a small open-fronted refrigerator. In it was a range of dairy and juice products.

Organic yoghurt – single	*£1.09*
Organic yoghurt x 4	*£2.89*
Fresh fruit smoothie – 250ml	*£1.99*
Fresh fruit smoothie – 1l	*£3.69*
Energy drink – single	*£1.15*
Energy drink x 4	*£3.95*
Chocolate teapot – single	*£1.59*
Chocolate teapot x 4	*£4.45*

I thought about it for a while. "I guess if I were in the habit of buying these kind of things the chocolate teapot would seem like reasonable value. How often do people buy a four-pack of Red Bull, though?"

Maggie opened up a notebook. "There are about two million cans of Red Bull sold every week in UK supermarkets, a million smoothies and – even more tempting – a hundred million pots of yoghurt. So it's not a bad market to get into."

I nodded.

"The point is, the positioning of the product makes a huge difference to how much people will pay for it. If we put it next to the teabags, people will compare it to the price of a teabag or a cup of coffee, which is between 3p and 10p. £2.79 for six seems hugely expensive. But if it's next to a freshly made cappuccino, you're willing to pay £2.89 for just one. A vast difference. We think the sweet spot for the supermarkets is in the fresh snack drink range, similar to a smoothie or a yoghurt, or a packaged hot chocolate. This lets us charge around £2. But there's clearly a market in the café sector too, so we will try to distribute it there as well."

As it turned out over the following months, the café market was a big one. It wasn't clear right away whether it was more valuable as a sales channel in itself, or as a way of creating product awareness for future purchases at the supermarket. In any case, once Maggie got one chain to sell the chocolate teapots, the others followed within six months.

When customers first encounter a new product or service, they usually have only the vaguest idea of what it is worth to them. In a few cases the product may have quantifiable material benefits — this is true of some financial services, and some business purchases. This gives a clear rationale for the price of the service — if something will make you £10,000 in profit, it is probably worth paying up to £9,000 for it.

Mostly, though, it is hard for us to know what we should pay for a product. We might try to predict the enjoyment we will get from consuming it. However, that is intrinsically difficult to guess — and even if we can, it doesn't naturally translate into a sum of money. Instead, we are likely to compare it with something similar we have encountered before and use that as a benchmark.

Imagine your friend from Estonia is visiting, and discovers that one of your neighbourhood pubs serves her favourite drink, which is made in Tallinn from local ingredients. You offer to buy her a glass of it. How much would you expect to pay?

Imagine it is poured from a bottle into a wine glass. You might compare it with wine, and expect to be charged £4 for 175ml. If it's poured into a champagne glass, it might be £7 for the same amount. If you instead discover that it is sold by the half pint, you are likely to compare it with beer, and £2 for the half pint will seem reasonable. If it is served in a shot glass, you would probably think of it as a liqueur and be happy to pay £2 for 25ml. That's a price difference of 11 times, just based on how the drink is presented. Of course the alcohol content is also a factor — but not a factor of 11.

Whichever products we most closely associate a new purchase with are the ones we are likely to use as a price guideline. Most products could potentially be compared with a number of different alternatives. The supplier therefore has the opportunity to shape our expectations by creating an association with a more expensive product.

Chocolate teapots might be seen as similar to teabags, or to freshly made cappuccinos from a coffee shop. The Estonian local tipple might be more like beer, more like whisky or more like champagne. And a service to complete your tax return could be compared with paying £5.50 for registered post, £95 for a software program or £2,000 for a bespoke service from a highly qualified professional.

The benefit matrix

Every product benefit can be seen in terms of something deeper.

Think about your product or service and all the benefits it provides. You should think hard to work out all the reasons somebody might buy from you. Then look in turn at each of those reasons and see if there is something more basic behind it. For instance, the taste of a drink might provide sweetness – which is a basic biological desire – and it might also provide familiarity, comfort and reminders of pleasant memories. These memories in turn can be broken down into something even more basic. Ultimately, every benefit is based on two fundamental emotional drives, pain and pleasure, and two fundamental material benefits, time and money (you can ultimately consider money and time also to be enablers of pleasure, but adding this extra level is not much help in practice).

For example, here's how it works for the Chocolate Teapot Company:

Primary (level 1) drivers	Level 2 drivers	Level 3 drivers	Basic drives
The taste of chocolate tea	Sweetness		Pleasure
	Energy from sugar		
	Memory associations		
Quenching thirst			Preventing pain

Satisfying a caffeine habit	Reducing tiredness	Productivity at work	Pleasure Increased wealth
The camaraderie of sharing a drink with someone	Social bonds		Pleasure

And here's an example for an accountancy firm:

Primary (level 1) drivers	Level 2 drivers	Level 3 drivers	Basic drives
Compliance with regulation	Reduced likelihood of fines and penalties	Direct cost savings	Money
	Reduced stress		Reduced pain
	Feelings of order		
	Doing the right thing for society	Sense of community	
Management information	Increased sense of control		Reduced pain
	Better planning	Profits	Money Pleasure
	Improved firm strategy		
Reduced tax bills	Cost saving		Money
	Cash flow improvement	Reduced stress	Reduced pain
		Greater ability to grow the business	Money Pleasure

At the end of the chapter there is a blank version of this table for you to fill in yourself.

This matrix of values shows all the different reasons – conscious and unconscious – that influence somebody to buy your service or product. In any given situation the customer will only consider a small number of these reasons, which is a powerful opportunity for you.

For each of these buying reasons, you have a different set of competitors. A customer has a number of choices they can make to satisfy each of these needs.

For example, a customer who wants to taste something sweet has various options apart from a chocolate teapot. They could also buy a packet of wine gums, or an ordinary cup of tea with sugar, or a dessert. Someone who just wants a hot drink could choose tea, coffee or hot chocolate. And someone who wants the social bond of sharing a drink could go to a café and share a coffee; they could go to the pub for a glass of wine; or they could even go to the cinema.

Each different set of competitors has its own price spectrum. If you make the right choice of competitor and choose your positioning accordingly, you can choose a completely different price point. This will transform your profitability.

The accounting firm described above might choose to focus on one key group of values: compliance (which largely covers doing the annual accounts and tax returns for small firms). If it did so, it would be stuck in a low-value market, being compared with self-employed bookkeepers and high-volume accounting 'factories' that have a low cost base and can undercut a traditional accounting firm. This is likely to be a low-profit option.

Alternatively, it could focus on tax consulting: a higher-value market and one where the price charged is easier to tie to the value generated (see the case studies in Chapter 15 for details). Tax consulting perhaps calls for more creativity, and as a result is a less price-competitive market.

The firm could position itself as a business adviser, offering strategic input into its clients' commercial and investment decisions. This decision can unlock high value, because some business decisions can make a difference of many millions of pounds in value; and if the firm plays an integral part in helping its client make the right decision, it can charge a price commensurate with the difference it makes.

However, this last option brings with it a different set of positioning considerations. The market for business advice services is much smaller than that for compliance services. The way a business advice firm needs to present itself to earn confidence from clients is very different from the way an accountant should behave. The firm needs to show the right kind of experience to gain credibility to provide such a service. And most businesses will resist the high fees that come with this service — at least they will if those fees are quoted in the traditional way.

Thus, a firm following this route should instead choose a pricing strategy that does not confront the client immediately with the cost of the service. The best way to do this is to charge a share of money the client doesn't yet have: the benefits of future growth. Firms should look at structures whereby they enter into a joint-venture or revenue-sharing arrangement with a client; where the firm's advice contributes to the success of a new growth market, the firm will end up with a stake in a far more valuable asset than they could ever have persuaded the client to pay in cash.

Many accountants hate this idea. It is more risky to enter into an equity-based or revenue-sharing relationship than to charge a fee in advance, since many client ventures will fail, or stagnate, and will not make much money for the accountant. It requires an investment of time up front while the return, if it ever comes, will be far in the future. It is an unusual approach, with few examples to copy from, and requires an entrepreneurial commitment from the professional that may not come naturally. But those who do it will make far more money than they could have done in the traditional way.

How to apply it

In the 'How to apply it' section of each chapter I will show you a process you can go through to use the insights of that chapter in your own business. The benefit matrix exercise in this chapter is the most important in the book, because the benefits and values of your product or service will then provide the basis for most of the other techniques in the later chapters. You can download more copies of this matrix from the website www. psyprice.com.

First, fill out the benefit matrix by analysing the benefits or value that your customers get from you. Write these benefits into column 1. Each direct benefit is likely to have something deeper underlying it, as shown in the examples above. Put these in column 2, and so on. Ultimately you will get down to the four basic drives: avoidance of pain; pleasure; time; and money.

You may find that there are either more or fewer than four levels of benefit; for example, you might go straight from level 2 drives to avoidance of pain and to pleasure. If you don't need column 2 or 3, just leave them blank. If you need more columns there are other versions of the table on the website.

Use the value comparison chart on page 14 to choose one of the key benefits (values) of your product, and write down as many other products as you can think of that provide the same benefit. Write down the typical price of the other products. You can then choose which of these competitors you want to position yourself against, and whether you would rather be seen as a teabag or as a freshly made cappuccino.

The 'units' column may be hard to fill in. For some products there is a clear unit of value. For example, with transport services it is the distance travelled; for accommodation, the number of nights stayed. Other products or services do not have clear units: for example, the brand value provided by a BMW definitely provides a benefit to the customer, but it is hard to imagine what units this could be measured in. You may be able to think of a way to represent it – perhaps the number of friends and acquaintances who will notice the brand? – but if not, then just leave the units column blank.

The example shown at the top of the chart is for a supplier of health drinks, who has found that its key customer benefits are *refreshment, self-image* (through the branding of its product) and *health* (through the vitamins and herbs infused in the drink). Please use the blank rows underneath to fill in your own examples, or download an electronic version from www.psyprice.com.

Once you have come up with a list of services or products that provide the same benefits as yours, you should be able to see which ones have the highest per-unit price. Consider how you can position yourself as an alternative to those: this is where you can probably achieve the highest price for your product.

The benefits or values which you choose to focus on – those which will position you against the highest-value competitors which therefore enable you to achieve the highest price – are called your **critical value dimensions.**

Bear in mind the likely sales volume of the products you are positioning against. If you position your new car model against Ferrari instead of against BMW, you can probably achieve a higher price per unit, but you will not sell as many cars. The next chapter shows you how to analyse the volume you need to sell.

Benefit matrix

Level 1 drivers (benefits)	Level 2 drivers (features)	Level 3 drivers (emotions)	Basic drives

Value comparison chart

Benefit or value (taken from any column of the benefit matrix)	Competitor	Units of value	Price per unit
Refreshment	Lager in pub	Minutes spent drinking	10p
	Sparkling water in café	Minutes spent drinking	12p
	Tap water at home	Minutes spent drinking	0p
Self-image	Alternative therapy session	Per session	£50
	Competitive health drinks	Per bottle	£2.50
	Reading a magazine	Per issue	£4
Health	Gym membership	Per session	£8
	Salad (in restaurant)	One salad	£6
	Salad (from supermarket)	One salad	£2

Benefit or value	Competitor	Units of value	Price per unit

Chapter summary

■ The value that customers place on your product is subjective, and influenced strongly by context.

■ You can increase this value – and the price customers are willing to pay – by positioning your product alongside a more expensive alternative.

■ To understand what alternatives customers might perceive as legitimate comparisons for your product, analyse the benefits it provides.

■ Each time you identify a benefit, ask yourself what deeper need that benefit fulfils, until you get right down to basic pleasure and pain.

■ These benefits will be a key tool in understanding the psychological pricing and marketing of your product or service.

Chapter 2

Cost-based calculations

Your baseline, not your price

The factory wasn't up and running yet, but Maggie took me to the food laboratory where the prototype teapots were being put together. I had to put on gloves, a protective hat and even disposable shoe covers for hygiene. Somehow the outfit seemed to suit her much better than me.

The manufacturing process was painstaking but not immensely complex. The plastic teapots were made in an injection mould, with the bowl of the pot emerging from the mould first and the spouts fitted and sealed in place afterwards. Then something that looked like a garden sprinkler sprayed a layer of liquid chocolate onto the inside of the pot. Leaves were sealed into a small teabag, which was dropped into the teapot once the chocolate had cooled down, with a thread attached and a tag hanging out of the lid.

Maggie was cautious when I asked her about the cost of the teapot.

"It depends on what you include in the cost. The individual ingredients are not too expensive once we have the equipment in place: the teapot costs about 5p, the chocolate 6p and the teabag about 3p. Plus another 5p or 10p depending on how we design the packaging. But it has cost us at least £30,000 to put all this equipment together just for the prototypes. And the real factory will be 10 times that – just to get a single production line running.

"The big question is marketing. If it catches on, we might get away without spending too much. If not, we may have to spend

three times as much selling it as we do making it. It's all quite unpredictable, which makes it hard to answer your question."

"So what's the least you could sell each teapot for?" I asked.

She paused. "That's not the kind of question that has a meaningful answer. If we sold just a pot on its own, perhaps about 20p . . . but then we have to make enough profit to pay back the cost of the equipment and marketing. That depends on whether we sell 10,000 or 100,000 pots."

"At least you can get a reliable 50% markup if you sell it at 30p, then . . ." Maggie shook her head, frowning, and I tailed off. Clearly she was reluctant to discuss it any more. The conversation left me wondering whether this company was going to be wildly profitable or struggling to pay the wages. With hindsight, I realise Maggie had no better idea of the answer than I did. What was clear was she was working as hard as I'd ever seen anyone work to get these products developed and sold.

In this chapter, we don't look much at psychology; rather, this is an analysis of some financial aspects of your business which will provide the baseline for psychological strategies in future chapters. So if you already know all about your fixed and variable costs, and your breakeven volume, you can just skim this chapter.

For many companies, examining their cost base is as far as they get towards determining a pricing strategy. It is an important step, but it is only a small part of the picture. The cost of providing your product or service tells you the lowest price you can charge, but it does not tell you the right price.

One reason for this is that the right price depends on the volume you sell. Your variable costs — the direct material costs of manufacturing each item or delivering each service — are incurred for each unit you sell. Your fixed costs are incurred when you start up or invest in expansion, and then each month while you operate. These fixed costs must be apportioned across all the units you sell to find the breakeven price — but you do not know in advance how many sales you will achieve. And the sales you can achieve are in turn influenced by the price point you set.

This makes the minimum price nearly impossible to calculate exactly. The calculation ends up being circular, and you can only work it out if you have an unachievable level of detail on customer buying behaviour.

However, you can at least work out some options. Here's an example for the Chocolate Teapot Company.

	Base costs		If they sell . . .		
			10 units/year	100,000 units/year	3m units/year*
Base (variable) cost per unit	19p		19p	19p	19p
Startup costs (over 3 years)	£330,000				
Startup cost apportioned per year	£110,000	Startup cost per teapot	£11,000	£1.10	3.7p
Annual costs – marketing plus overheads	£250,000	Overheads per teapot	£25,000	£2.50	8.3p
Minimum selling price per unit			**£36,000.19**	**£3.79**	**31p**

* In fact, if they sell as many as three million units, the company will probably have to invest in more equipment, and overheads will go up to support the extra sales and distribution. The fixed costs will therefore increase, but as they buy in bulk and get better prices on the ingredients, variable costs will go down. The minimum selling price will probably go down a little overall.

You can see how much the minimum selling price varies depending on the volume you sell. This makes it very important to get some idea of the volume you can expect, so that you know what kinds of positioning are compatible with your costs.

In this example, CTC knows that they cannot pursue a high-volume positioning strategy that puts them in competition with teabags and instant coffee. If they had not been confident of selling at least a million units, it would have been impossible to sell into the supermarket channel at all – they would have had to restrict themselves to cafés only.

This information gives you some important input into your strategy and a check on your cost structure, but it is only the very beginning of your pricing journey. Do not be tempted to take your costs and simply add on a percentage for profit. You will be leaving money on the table but, more importantly, you will be sending the wrong signals to your customers.

If all you value about your product is the ingredients that go into it, you will signal to your customers that there is little reason to buy from you, except to save themselves the trouble of putting the ingredients together on their own. To give your customers something to believe in, a reason to buy from you as well as a reason to pay attention to the experience of consuming your product or service – and to make a profit that is worth the time and passion you put into your business – you must find a way to charge a price based on the value you give to your customer, and not the cost you incur in doing it.

How to apply it

To work out your minimum selling price, fill out the following tables:

Direct cost per unit

Direct labour cost 1	
Direct labour cost 2	
Direct labour cost 3	
Material cost 1	
Material cost 2	
Material cost 3	
Material cost 4	
Material cost 5	
TOTAL (a)	

Fixed costs

Startup capital – one-off costs (b)	
Management salaries	
Marketing salaries	
Operational salaries	
Marketing costs	
Office/premises rental	
Other overheads	
Other	
TOTAL (c)	

	Base costs	If you sell . . .		
		____ units/year	____ units/year	____ units/year
Per unit	(a)			
Startup costs (over ____ years)	(b)			
Startup cost per year				
Annual costs – marketing plus overheads	(c)			
Minimum selling price per unit				

Chapter summary

- Your costs should not be the main basis of your price, but they do provide a baseline for the minimum you can afford to charge.

- Understanding the difference between fixed and variable costs is critical to knowing how to maximise the profits from a product.

- All prices must cover variable costs, but some pricing strategies are specifically designed to help cover your fixed costs.

In focus

Famous prices in history

In the history books, a price may seem like just another number. In fact, there were many negotiations in past centuries in which the price was critical, not just to the deal itself, but also in how it was seen by posterity.

- What is now the state of Alaska was sold by Russia to America in 1867 for two cents per acre, or a total of $7.2m. Russia wanted to get rid of it as it feared it might lose the land anyway in future wars; the purchase was mostly seen as positive by Americans, except for those who realised that the cost of maintaining and policing the land might far exceed the purchase price. As things transpired, the oil and minerals under the land are incredibly valuable, and their exploitation is now a politically controversial topic in the USA. What's more, without Alaska we would never have had Sarah Palin.

- The Louisiana Purchase was even more significant. Nearly a quarter of the current land in the USA, covering 15 states, was purchased from France for $15m in 1803. The history of this purchase and its consequences had immense significance for the future of the USA – and France treated its sale as a political gain – helping establish the USA as a naval power that would potentially rival Britain.

- London Bridge was sold as a tourist attraction to a US property developer for £1.6m in 1968. Despite popular myth, it is apparently not true that the buyer thought he was getting Tower Bridge. It is hard to evaluate whether this price was a good deal for the buyer – it turned out he had to build his own bridge anyway and could use only the marble stone facing from the original – but no doubt it helped to establish the reputation of his tourist resort in Arizona. London County Council had decided to demolish the bridge anyway, so whatever price they managed to get for it was better than nothing.

■ In an early value-based pricing deal, Christopher Columbus agreed with Queen Isabella of Spain that he (and his funders) would receive 10% of all revenues from whatever new lands he discovered in his explorations. Perhaps unsurprisingly, the Queen reneged on this part of their deal.

■ The price of oil may be the most important single price in history. It has been a driver of much of political and economic history from the 1970s onwards. The oil supply crises of the 1970s pushed the price of oil to a record high, which led directly to military conflicts in the Middle East, helped Keynesian fiscal policy to fall out of favour, and contributed to the political history of the 1980s and 1990s in the USA and Europe. The rise of oil prices in 2007 and 2008 to a new record of $145 per barrel probably contributed to the financial crisis and recession that started in the latter year. Though many people think that conspiracies between suppliers help to push prices up, it seems unlikely that the oil market, which is worth $3 trillion a year, could possibly be manipulated in this way. This may be the least psychologically driven price there is, although the psychology of how consumers and politicians respond to it could be the subject of a whole new book.

■ The price of gold used to be of huge political significance, but it is now much less important. Gold (and silver) was used to set the effective value of most currencies until the 1930s, and in some countries up to the 1970s. The gold standard meant that the price of gold – legally defined as $20.67 per ounce in the USA until the 1930s – limited the number of dollars or pounds that a government could issue. Most economists believe that the gold standard, and the resulting lack of flexibility in monetary policy, helped cause the Great Depression. When the USA revalued gold to $35 per ounce in 1934, and the UK left the gold standard altogether, both economies started to recover.

■ More generally, governments have often tried to fix the price of goods, usually by forbidding suppliers from raising prices beyond a certain level. Typically this is done because demand exceeds supply at the current price, and rather than allowing prices to rise, the policy instead causes supply shortages which can only be solved by queues or rationing. This typically affects basic commodities such as bread and petrol, though some governments in the 1960s and 1970s tried to freeze prices and wages across their whole economy to control inflation.

■ The price of the Imperial Palace in Tokyo and the three square miles around it was once famously estimated at more than the value of all the land in California. Of course, it was never sold at this price; it is reasonable to think that if this much land had come onto the market in Tokyo, land prices would have fallen substantially.

■ Manhattan, on the other hand, really was sold. Dutch colonists bought it for 60 guilders in 1626 from Native Americans who lived next door in Brooklyn. Exchange rates were not really established at that time, but the value has been estimated at about $1,000. If invested for the 386 years since, at 4% interest, that money would now be worth $3.75bn – quite cheap, though considering the land was undeveloped at the time, maybe not a complete rip-off of the locals. If they could have got 6% interest, their $1,000 would have turned into nearly $6 trillion – at which price the seller definitely got the best end of the deal.

■ Maybe the most famous sale in history is the 30 pieces of silver that the Bible says was paid by the priests to Judas to betray Jesus. Historically this may be related to the standard price paid for a slave – some prices in ancient times were much more stable than they are today, as inflation did not really exist. A myriad of prices are defined in various cultures as amounts to be paid for certain things: a day of labour, the punishment for putting out someone's eye, and many more. Anthropologist David Graeber suggests that these legally defined prices are the reason why debts and money were originally invented, and that trade and other uses of money only emerged afterwards.

Chapter 3

Reading the customer's mind

Price discrimination and letting people tell you what they want

One windy Saturday morning in May 2009 I arrived to see Maggie lining up a number of teapots on a long dining table. She'd invited me along to see some of the first customer tests of the new products. The key question today was: how much should she charge for a chocolate teapot?

The traditional approach to this question is to work out a "demand curve". It's obvious that people will buy more if the product is cheaper, and less if it is more expensive. But if you make it too cheap, the lost profit margins may outweigh the additional volume. And if it's too expensive, you might sell none at all, or too few to be worthwhile. Somewhere along the price range there is an optimal, most profitable price. And to find out what that is, you either need to do lots of customer surveys, or try it out in the shops, and see how much people are willing to spend.

The diagrams on the next page show what a traditional demand curve looks like, with various different price points.

The standard economic reasoning goes like this: no matter what price you are charging now, if you increase the price you'll sell less, and if you cut the price you'll sell more. At some point when you cut the price too much, you won't win enough new sales to make up for it, and the total revenue will fall (which you see at the £2 price level in diagram 1 on the next page). Similarly, if you increase the price too much, you will lose more

Diagram 1

Diagram 2

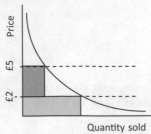

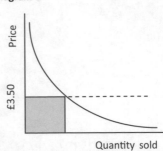

customers than are justified by the extra revenue (£5 in this example). But at some point in the middle, there's an optimal price where you earn the maximum revenue – the point where the rectangle under the curve has the largest area (as shown in diagram 2). (In fact you want to maximise profit instead of revenue, but the argument works the same way.)

I asked Maggie if she already had some idea what the demand curve for chocolate teapots might be like, and she laughed.

"Demand curves? Demand curves are useless. Let me show you why."

The first four customers had come in and started to look at the teapots on display. They each picked out a teapot and wrote down how much they'd be willing to pay for it. One of Maggie's researchers collected up the slips of paper and handed them over to her. She showed them to me:

- £1.15

- £2.10

- 99p

- 40p

"Right," said Maggie, "so how much should we charge per teapot if we want to make the most profit from these four customers? Ignore the manufacturing costs for now – you can assume it only costs a few pennies to make."

I tried to figure it out. "Well, probably not 40p. You would sell one to all four customers but you'd only get £1.60 in total. And if you charge £2.10 you'd get more than that from the second customer alone."

"Good. So what if we pick a price in between?"

"Well, if we go for £1.15 we will sell one to each of the first two customers, for £2.30. And if we go for 99p we'll make £2.97. So that seems to be the best option."

"OK, well done. That is the right answer according to the demand curve. And it's completely wrong according to me. Here's why."

Maggie called over the third customer, who'd written down 99p. His name tag said "John".

"Hey, John. So you're willing to pay 99p for a teapot." John nodded. "Thanks, that's good to know. Unfortunately we've been looking at the figures and we are not sure we can make it profitable at that price. Do you think you'd be able to stretch to £1.10?"

John thought about it a bit. "Yeah, probably. It's only 10p more; I suppose that doesn't make much difference. I'm pretty curious to try it out and see what it tastes like."

Maggie thanked him, and John continued. "Are you really going to make these things? It seems a ridiculous idea."

Maggie laughed. "Well, let's see if we can make this work. I think you'll like it once you give it a try."

John went back to the table and Maggie turned to me. "So, there's your first problem with the demand curve: customers don't tell you the truth. They tell you a lower figure than they are really willing to pay, because they want to get you to set a lower price. They think if they give you a low answer, they'll be able to buy it cheaper when you launch. In fact, they probably don't even know what they're really willing to pay: it's influenced by how much you ask for the product, what else is sitting around them in the shop, what mood they're in – lots of things that they can't control and aren't even aware of a lot of *the time. And if we can figure out that John will really pay £1.10, we can set the price accordingly and make £3.30 total revenue, 10% more than we thought originally."*

"But isn't that always a problem with measuring people in a lab?" I asked. "Presumably if you go out and get real sales data by testing the product in a shop, you can get the truth?"

"Well, you can get closer to it. But every shop is different, and the truth when you test a new product is different from the truth after it's been launched, advertised, people get to know it and the novelty effect wears off. So you have to make some kind of compromise between what people tell you, what you can infer from the products they buy in shops today, and your vision for what you have invented. In any case, that's not the biggest problem with the demand curve approach. Let me show you something else."

Maggie asked the second customer, who'd written down £2.10, to come over and talk to us. Her tag said "Elise".

"Hi, Elise. Thanks for coming in today. We're looking at launching these new teapots in the next two months and so your input is really important to us. Now let me ask you a question. You've said you'd be willing to spend £2.10 on a teapot, and that's roughly the price we are expecting to launch it at. But what if the usual price was £2.10 in the shop you normally visit, but on the way there you noticed teapots on sale at another shop for £1.10. Do you think you'd continue on to your usual shop?"

"Well, no, of course not," Elise replied. "Why would I pay more if it was available for a pound less?"

"Sure. So let's say you go into the store and it turns out the £1.10 version is a smaller pot and the chocolate isn't your favourite kind. What is your favourite, by the way?"

"I like the bitter kind – Green & Black's is what I usually buy."

"OK, so this one is a Cadbury's Dairy Milk teapot. Still interested?"

"Not sure – I suppose it depends on my mood. But I'd probably give it a miss and buy the one I originally wanted."

Maggie thanked her and walked outside with me.

"So here's the main point about demand curves. You have a customer there who's ready and willing to hand over £2.10 to you. But if you set your price at £1.10 – sure, you'll get John and the other guy to buy from you, but you're giving free money to Elise. She told us she'll pay £2.10, but if we offer it for less, of course she'll take it for less."

"So what are you going to do? If you sell it for £2.10 you'll lose the business of the other two."

"Indeed. What we really want to do is find out from each customer, as they walk into the shop, how much they are willing to pay. Then set the price to exactly that amount. That way, we'll get the maximum amount from each customer. We might even be able to win over the 40p customer as well, if we can manufacture the product for less than that. If we can do that, we'll make £4.75 from these four customers – 50% more than we first thought."

I protested that this was ridiculous. "Nobody's going to tell you what they're willing to pay and wait for you to change the price tag. Why would they? And anyway the shops aren't going to run around and retag the product for every customer."

Maggie nodded. "Absolutely not. But this is where we can be clever. The reason that Elise is willing to pay more than the others is that she puts a higher value on some aspects of the teapot than they do. If we can find out what those are, we can make different teapots for each customer, and each of those can have a different price. We can make a Green & Black's teapot for Elise, a Dairy Milk teapot for John and a 'Basics' own-brand teapot for Mr 40p. Each customer pays the appropriate price and we get maximum revenue."

"And what if the person who'll pay £2.10 actually prefers Dairy Milk?"

"We need to find another aspect of quality that they value more. We can still make a high-quality milk chocolate version. Or maybe a luxury brand image will appeal to them, or a larger size pot. That's what our market research will help us find out.

"We are looking into people's minds and getting them to reveal what they're thinking, not by telling us directly, but by which product variation they choose to buy."

Case study

Cereals at Tesco

In researching this chapter I visited my local Tesco. It's a large store so has a wide range of products. Certain categories are highly prone to price discrimination. I picked breakfast cereals.

A box of cereal is available for as little as 31p (Everyday Value Corn Flakes) or as much as £4.39 (Jordans Super 3-Seed Granola). Each of these gives approximately 15 servings, so they are roughly comparable.

This doesn't show what an economist would call 'pure' price discrimination – where you charge different prices for exactly the same product – but that is very rare. In reality, people who are willing to pay more do get a better product: undoubtedly the Jordans cereal is tastier and, if you care about organic food, it's better on that dimension too. But the key principle is there: Tesco doesn't lose the custom of people who don't value their cereal much, or can't afford Jordans. But they also don't lose the extra profits from the wealthier customers who are willing to spend more for quality.

Those in the middle get to buy Kellogg's Crunchy Nut Cornflakes at £2.68, Tesco Blueberry Wheats at £1.75 or Country Barn Maple and Pecan Crisp at £1.05. And those who are on a very tight weekly budget and don't even want to spend 89p can get a mini box of Basics cornflakes for just 65p. There is a product for everyone, wherever they are on the willingness-to-pay spectrum.

Maggie's method works in every kind of business. Nearly every market contains a range of customers: some who are willing to pay more, either because they value the product more highly or simply because they have more money; and others who are willing or able to pay less. If you sell a standardised product, you can use Maggie's method of product differentiation to extract more money from higher-end clients.

It's even easier if you are preparing bespoke quotations for each prospect, say if you're a lawyer or a consultant. You can simply put a different price on each service according to what you think the customer will pay. You may not know this for every client, though. Sometimes the prospect has a budget and they won't tell you. Or sometimes, like John, the client may not really know what they are willing to pay until they see what is on offer.

For these clients you can do what Maggie does with the teapots: offer a range of different options and let the client self-select into their budget category. You may have a rough idea – for instance in a public tender, the client may tell you they expect to spend £50,000–£100,000 (or you may know this because of the way in which they announce the tender – if they invite competitive quotes but do not advertise it formally in the relevant official publications). Then you can pitch three options to cover this range. Or you may have no idea at all, in which case you can design a wider range of packages covering a broad price range.

The demand curve now looks like this:

Diagram 3

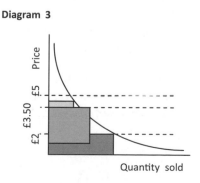

Instead of earning the revenue in just one of the three rectangles, you can earn the combined area of all three. Often this results in an increase of up to 50% in total income.

The difference between this and the anchoring approach is that, in this case, the customer already has some idea of what they are willing to pay, but you don't know what it is. Anchoring is more useful when the customer has no idea at all and you want to shape their expectations.

Some companies, when using this technique, sell the lower-cost products under a different brand. This is especially visible in the fashion industry, where top designers (Giorgio Armani, Donna Karan) will launch 'diffusion' brands that may refer to their name but are clearly distinct (Emporio Armani, DKNY). Sophisticated buyers know that the original brand is designed and manufactured independently from the diffusion brand, and the existence of the cheaper product does not damage the brand image, but the diffusion label still borrows some of the cachet of the original name.

Case study

Jewellery maker

LM, a jeweller, has two distinct customer groups: individuals who wear his pieces; and retailers who sell them. For simplicity we will focus on the individuals: small shops are often content to simply set a retail price which is double the wholesale price, so LM has a lot of control over the end-price offered to consumers even via the retail channel.

Jewellery is valued in part according to the rarity of the materials used – diamonds are more expensive than rubies, and platinum costs more than silver. However, materials costs make up only a small share of the price of most pieces, so the real determinants of price are the designers' and makers' skills.

This creates an opportunity to shape the perceived value of each object through pricing.

We start, as usual, with an analysis of the consumer's values.

- Making myself look beautiful.

- Impressing my partner with a thoughtful gift.

- Showing off to my friends.

- Creating a token of our memories.

- Acting as a symbol of our relationship.

Each of these can be communicated or reinforced with a particular pricing choice.

Let's take as an example 'Making myself look beautiful'. Often this value is satisfied by proxy – a person may buy a bracelet or necklace for their partner in the hope that the partner will like it. There is a great deal of uncertainty for many people in making a purchase like this; they feel unsure about whether their partner will actually like the piece.

Price is a good way to provide implicit reassurance that they will. The jeweller, while not knowing the personal taste of the recipient, is in a good position to know what customers in general are likely to like. So LM creates a hierarchy of products – in the bracelet case, starting at £120 and going up to £250, £390 and £750. He decides to decorate the cheapest bracelet with fussy and inelegant flourishes to make it clear that this bracelet, although it's available if you really want it, is not the right choice for someone who wants to impress their new lover.

As price goes up, the aesthetic initially becomes simpler and more classic, with subtle details introduced at the high end – details which add nuance and distinction to the design, but are inconspicuous enough to avoid ostentation.

A lot of buyers who are not confident to make a decision purely on aesthetic value will be guided by the pricing structure into an understanding of which bracelets are regarded as the most beautiful. In case anyone does not get the message, the £120 bracelet is originally sold at £140 and clearly marked down to £120. Similarly, the £250 piece is reduced from £290.

A money-back offer is available on full-priced merchandise, so that if the recipient doesn't like it, it is easy to return it and choose an alternative. However, this offer is not available on sale items – and thus the buyer who wants to be absolutely certain has another reason to choose a higher-end product.

To support the price distinction it is important that other product attributes are consistent with the pricing message. Thus the £750 bracelet contains platinum, or a higher grade of gold, and is heavier. The £120 bracelet might be silver, or a thin, light and slightly flimsy gold band.

Some suppliers do not like the idea of making a product which is deliberately designed to be less attractive than their premium offer. However, it can be shown in economic theory that this approach achieves the best combination of price and quality to make the products available to as many people as possible.

LM decided to use a different brand name on the £120 bracelet, in order to maintain the exclusivity of his name, and to more strongly define the expensive items as high-quality pieces. This is a good approach to positioning, and keeps his options open for mass-market sales of the lower-quality brand – a diffusion label – if he should choose to pursue that strategy later.

How to apply it

To use this technique with your own products, you need to figure out two things. First, what is the range of willingness to pay across your potential customer base? Second, what factors do they value which you can use to customise and differentiate your product range?

Both of these can be estimated by talking to customers. In my own work, I use different interviewing techniques to elicit what people are really willing to spend – just asking them the question is unlikely to get at the real answer. There are some examples of these interviews in the next chapter, and at www.psyprice.com. You can also find out on the website how to get in touch with me if you'd like to find out more.

Working out what customers value is sometimes easier – you can do a lot of this yourself by just putting yourself in the customer's place and thinking about why they might buy your product or service. This process is called **value modelling** and it is a basic step for many of the techniques in this book, so I recommend you do it either now or soon, before testing out some of the more advanced approaches. You can use the table on page 39 to record the values that your customers hold.

Once you've filled in some initial values, try bringing this table to some customers or potential customers and talking through their reasons for buying your product or service. They'll probably come up with some values or benefits you hadn't thought of before. And if they mention ones that you already have, put a mark in the second column so that you have a record of how often people mentioned this particular value (see the example on page 38). This will give you an idea of how important it is and to how many customers.

Talk first to them without showing them the table, so you get their unprompted thoughts. Then if the conversation runs out of steam, you can show them the table and see which of the values you already have written down they agree with. Be warned – you will probably get more than you expect! Most times when I do this exercise with a business we come up with 20 to 30 values on our own, before we have even spoken to their customers.

After this, you should take the top answers – usually the top five or so – to a new set of potential customers and ask them what kind of product they would associate with those benefits. In the example below, with top-quality chocolate and luxury brand image, they might talk about Green & Black's or Godiva chocolates. This will give you an indication of the price level you can charge.

Next, pick various subsets of the benefits that will fit naturally into a differentiated product range. Think about designing product or service packages that emphasise different combinations of the benefits. For instance, perhaps the top benefits of your chocolate are that it tastes good, feels like an indulgence, is fair to cocoa bean farmers, and is friendly to the environment. You could design a more expensive product which emphasises the luxury aspect, with better packaging and tasting notes. You could develop a version with an extra subsidy to the farmer – a 'super-Fairtrade' version. Or you could sell a non-organic version for more price-sensitive customers.

Value	Frequency
Quality of chocolate	llll
Luxury brand image	ll

Value	Frequency

Chapter summary

■ Different customers have different budgets, which are reflected in the amount they are willing to pay for your product.

■ To maximise your profits, and ensure that more customers have access to your products, you should design a range of prices so that those customers willing to pay more can pay more. This is called **price differentiation** or **price discrimination**.

■ In order to encourage better-off customers to pay more, you should differentiate the products and offer a more expensive version that is more attractive to them.

■ To work out how to differentiate the products, look at the values or benefits that the product gives to your customers, and design product versions that provide different amounts of those benefits.

■ You may have to deliberately reduce the appeal of the cheaper versions of your product in order to encourage wealthier customers to pay for the expensive version.

Chapter 4
Segmentation

'Customers don't know what they feel, don't say what they know, and don't do what they say. Market research is three steps removed from real behaviour.'

Ascribed to David Ogilvy, founder of advertising agency Ogilvy and Mather

I next saw Maggie on a street corner in the City of London.

She'd asked me to meet her there to watch her interviewing people as they passed – and while I waited for her to finish with some real customers, I decided to try answering her questionnaire myself.

1. How often do you drink tea?
   Once every two or three days

2. What kinds of tea do you normally drink?
   Breakfast tea, sometimes Darjeeling. Occasionally peppermint

3. Where do you buy your tea?
   Sainsbury's or Costa

4. What are the experiences or feelings you most associate with drinking tea?
   A nice relaxing drink before bed. Or something to drink at work when I've had too much coffee already

41

5. If you decided not to have a cup of tea, what might you have instead?
   Decaf coffee

6. What do you eat or drink alongside tea?
   Bacon roll. Or a croissant

7. Here's £10. If I asked you to go and spend some of it on buying tea, where would you go?
   Starbucks, probably

8. How much would you expect to pay for it there?
   £1.40, perhaps?

Over the next half an hour I watched some people answering the last couple of questions. Maggie was moving back and forth between two adjacent streets, and it was noticeable how much the answers were influenced by where people were standing. On one street there was a branch of Tesco, and people tended to point to it when offered their £10 note. On the next street there was no supermarket, but there was a Starbucks across the road. And most people on that street said they would buy at Starbucks.

Maggie explained: "Most people don't have strong opinions or even very clear memories of the products they buy. So it's quite easy to influence their answers by changing the way you ask a question or the environment they are in. In fact, one of the things that market research can best measure is not the actual answers to the questions, but how easy it is to influence the decisions people make."

"So if you figure out that 60% of people will change their answer according to which street they're standing in . . ." I started to ask.

". . . then we know that's how many people are likely to be susceptible to being pointed towards one shop or another to buy the product," she replied. "Quite useful to help us design our promotional offers or adverts."

Over the course of the day Maggie had collected about 40 questionnaires, and she said there were another 200 back at

the office. The next week we met again and she showed me
some of the results.

Segment	Willingness to pay	Other attributes
1	5p–15p	Never buy tea outside the office or home; always brew it themselves
2	50p–75p	Tend to like "builder's tea" with sugar – use as a morning stimulant
3	£1–£1.50	Regular drinkers, sometimes a few cups a day
4	£2–£3.50	Luxury teas – chai latte or specialist herbal/floral teas

"For now we're going to focus on these top two segments.
Looks like there are different product types that will work for
each – we may use different kinds of chocolate and definitely
different kinds of tea. There's no point in going for the lower
end right now. Maybe later we can work out how to develop a
product for them, but at the moment, anything we offer at
those price points will probably just lose sales from segments 3
and 4."

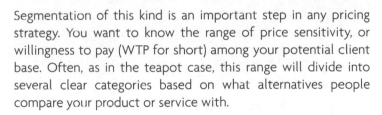

Segmentation of this kind is an important step in any pricing strategy. You want to know the range of price sensitivity, or willingness to pay (WTP for short) among your potential client base. Often, as in the teapot case, this range will divide into several clear categories based on what alternatives people compare your product or service with.

It is hard to span distinct WTP categories with a single product. If you are able to attract a customer base at £2.50, it's dangerous to also offer a 30p version of your product – customers might trade down, and the profits you lose on the £2.50 client will be hard to make up unless you can sell huge volumes of the cheaper version.

The more unusual your product is, the more you should aim for a premium price segment; if you have close competitors you may have to hit a particular price point to capture a volume market, but if not, the cons usually outweigh the pros.

Determining the segments of your potential customers is important but not easy. If you rely on looking at existing customer behaviour, you don't measure whether people would really be willing to pay more. If you speak to people who aren't your customers at present, you are asking them to think about a hypothetical situation and this makes it hard for them to give you accurate answers.

This is why questions like 7 and 8 in Maggie's questionnaire are important. Question 7 puts people in a situation which is relatively similar to the real buying environment, and asks them to make a real decision. This prompts the customer to go through at least some of the same mental processes that they go through when buying a real product. Having done that, the price point they think in response to question 8 is more likely to be accurate, and to reflect what they might really be willing to pay for the product.

It's risky to ask direct questions such as 'How much would you be willing to pay for this?' Apart from the difficulty for the consumer of trying to predict their potential behaviour in a hypothetical situation, many people will deliberately give you an underestimate – in some kind of strategic attempt to influence you to lower your prices. As far as you can, you should structure your questions to replicate the real process and mindset of a consumer buying a product.

How to apply it

You can use the following questionnaire as a starting point, but feel free to modify it. Identify different groups of people whom you think might have a different attitude to your product, or use it differently. Then speak to as many individuals as possible. You should target at least 10 in each group, though you can probably benefit from talking to more than that if you have the time and patience to do so.

Remember the David Ogilvy quote at the opening of this chapter. Your customers do not necessarily know, and will not necessarily say, what they would do when presented with your product in a real environment. Therefore, try to ask the question in such a way as to make the scenario as realistic as you can. Some techniques for doing this include the following.

- Ask the person to place themselves in the shoes of a third party – for instance, to predict what their friend would do instead of what they themselves would do. This creates distance, takes away a source of bias and a degree of subjectivity that might result in a false answer to the question if they tried to imagine their own behaviour.

- Give them some money and ask them to spend it on products in your category. Although this isn't perfect – because people treat newly acquired money in a different way from their own money, and because they might feel a moral obligation to buy a product they wouldn't normally want – it makes things much more realistic than simply asking the consumer to imagine how they might behave.

- Put them in a physical environment which is appropriate to the decision you want them to make. For example, when interviewing people about a luxury housekeeping service, I booked the interviews in a five-star hotel in central London in order to convey the brand values that I wanted to present. When interviewing about a new coffee product, try asking people in a café.

Questionnaire template

You should modify this to reflect your particular product or service. See the teapot questionnaire above for an example of how to do this.

- How often do you buy (or use) this type of product or service?

- What variety, or which brands, do you normally buy?

- Where do you buy it?

- What are the experiences or feelings you most associate with using this product?

- If you decided not to buy this particular product today, what might you buy instead?

- What do you buy, or use, alongside this product?

- If I gave you £10 [or an appropriate amount] and asked you to go and spend some of it on buying this product, where would you go?

- How much would you expect to pay for it when you got there?

Chapter summary

- Asking questions of your customers or potential customers is an important way to get insight into what they will spend money on.

- However, you can't take the answers literally. The responses customers give will indicate what they really think, but you have to read between the lines.

- One of the most important insights you will gain is what kind of questions or what context will *change* the answers that people give. This gives you a clue to how you can influence their decisions.

In focus

Does 99p pricing work?

Many of the prices in the examples so far have ended in 9. Does this really matter?

We all know that lots of products, from the sandwiches you buy for lunch up to a stereo, are priced with a 99p ending. Sometimes even a £24,000 car is priced at £23,999. Even this book is at a price point of £14.99. Surely this must make a big difference to sales?

The research literature says yes, but there are conflicting stories about how the practice originated and why it works. One story that goes around is that this originated not to increase sales, but to protect shops against embezzlement by their staff. If a customer paid $1 for a 99 cent item, the cashier would have to open the till to make change. In order to do so, they would be required to ring up the sale, preventing them from pocketing the dollar.

There is little evidence for this story, but it has the appeal of sounding plausible.

A more convincing psychological explanation is that people group prices into rough bands and apply very crude pattern-matching rules to make their decisions easier. Therefore a £2.99 sandwich falls into the '£2ish' band, while a £3.05 sandwich would be placed in the '£3ish' band and might be subconsciously excluded from the buyer's consideration. Supporting this, one experiment by Robert Schindler asked people to compare two products priced at $20 and $25; the difference in value was perceived as small. When the prices were reduced by one cent to $19.99 and $24.99, the difference was perceived as much greater and people were much more likely to choose the cheaper option.

There is some support for this in the evidence that people can subconsciously recognise a number without knowingly registering it. An amusing example is an experiment by Katherine Hahn at Michigan Business School. She presented subjects with two very similar options, for instance two erasers which were almost identical except for a few random marks or a corner that had been rubbed off. Unprompted, people were equally likely to choose either option. But when the two erasers were placed on either side of a large number 9, people were much more likely to choose the one on the right. When the number was 1, they chose the eraser on the left. Nothing else was changed except the number – and the hypothesis is that people subconsciously map the world onto a left-to-right one-to-10 number line, with digits providing cues for us to look left or right on this line. It is not known whether the effect is reversed in cultures where the language is written from right to left!

Overall, experience suggests that 99p price points do work. When your product is likely to be compared with a competitor's, cutting that extra penny off the price could make people more likely to buy it. When the customer is choosing between different options within your product range (such as on a menu in a restaurant) the 99p may be more likely to bias them to pick one of your cheaper options, which could be counterproductive.

Chapter 5
New launches, belief and fairness

Consumers were easy compared to the next group Maggie had to persuade: the buyers in the supermarket and café chains.

I was allowed to sit in on two of those meetings, and – though I'm not free to talk about the negotiations in detail – I can report my surprise at the cynicism of some buyers.

"You'll never sell them at that price," was the most common message. "It's a tea, it has to be priced in line with our teas," said the cafés. "We can't put this on the same shelf as a box of 40 PG Tips for the same price as one teapot," said the supermarkets.

The consumer research data helped but did not entirely persuade them – it is hard to change a person's firmly held beliefs with mere information.

The supermarket buyer claimed he could only sell a four-pack of teapots for £1.20, which would require CTC to price them at less than 20p per teapot. The café chain was a little more ambitious, suggesting a retail price of £1.40 for a single teapot, but with the higher margins that the café insisted on, this would still have forced CTC down to a 35p wholesale price point.

Maggie decided to take some risks. When one of the big four supermarkets refused to stock any teapots without a 50% cut from the original asking price, she stood up and left the room. It was clearly a tough decision so early in the life of the business, but doing it put her in a powerful position to negotiate with the other chains.

She went back into those negotiations and promised to take back unsold stock if it didn't sell at the listed prices. That, combined with an agreement to participate in several sales promotions during the first six months of the launch, did the trick. Once the first supermarket placed an order, the two others soon followed.

The following week, the first café chain, a subsidiary of consumer products giant Leverkraft & Gamble, agreed to add teapots to their menu in six stores.

1 September was chosen as the launch date, and everyone held their breath.

Persuading people in your industry that you are worth what you say can be one of the hardest tasks. Typically, they think they know more about pricing than they do. The typical mindset is to remember the last time they had a tough price negotiation with a client, and focus on that as if it represents the whole market. However, the very fact that it was a tough negotiation means the client was probably at the most price-sensitive end of the spectrum.

People do tend to assume that their most memorable experiences are the most typical ones (this is known as the **availability bias**). You would like them to look dispassionately across the whole market, but it is hard to persuade people to do that.

Negotiating with someone like this is especially difficult, because they will claim (and usually believe) that they are not negotiating on their own account, but simply reflecting their understanding of how much their customers are willing to pay. The supermarket that insists that their customers won't perceive your teapot as a premium product and the consultant who says that the client will pay no more than £600 a day for your expertise are probably both basing their opinion on the same lack of hard data.

A related argument you will sometimes hear is the **just price** – the idea that the prices you charge should be some kind of fair balance between your costs, the time you spend sourcing and distributing a product, and the demand for it. This concept goes all the way back to St Thomas Aquinas in the 13th century. We all want the prices we pay to be fair; but many people are unwilling to confront a supplier directly and suggest that they should be charged less. However, a third party who places themselves in the position of defending the end customer's interests, and who is probably more informed than the consumer about the margins you are likely to be making, might try to argue for fairness on the customer's behalf.

Modern economic theory puts little stock in the idea of fairness, but customers do like to be treated fairly. Therefore it is always worth having a rationale for your prices which you are happy to defend to customers. This will also be useful in negotiations with third parties or resellers. They may feel reassured to have ammunition in case their customers ask them about the basis of your prices. In reality, few customers will, but you may as well help assuage your partners' worries if you want to keep working with them.

A final danger for many new companies is the risk that their belief in their own value is undermined. This is the most common pitfall for individuals who set up as consultants or freelancers: they find it hard to believe that their time could possibly be worth hundreds or even thousands of pounds per day. This isn't the place for a seminar in self-confidence, but you can remind yourself of a few key facts.

- The value you offer to your client for a few hours of expertise could be immense – you are entitled to a fair share of it.

- By charging too little, you signal to your client that your advice is not worth much – this makes them less likely to follow it. Is that in their interest?

- There are always people in the market more expensive than you, and there is always somebody cheaper. Place yourself where you think you deserve to be – are you in the top 20% of people with your expertise? (You probably should be.)

Ultimately, you need to be willing to take responsibility for your prices: if you are firm in your conviction of your worth, you will be able to persuade customers to pay for your value and your positioning. You might need to help your partners to communicate that value with marketing support, or by giving them a clear script to follow when selling on your behalf. If you take control of that process, they are more likely to go along with you.

Case study

A specialist consultancy and its reseller

A specialist leadership training consultancy, McComb Associates, sometimes sold its services directly to clients but was more often used as a subcontractor by a larger management consulting firm, which I'll call Excisient. The large firm had its own standard pricing approach, based on charging its clients for their consultants' time at between £600/day and £1,000/day.

One of Excisient's clients was an international bank which brought in the consultants to help launch a new venture in China. Part of the work involved training top European executives to manage Chinese staff and communicate with Chinese government officials, and Excisient asked McComb to help with this.

McComb realised that the value to the bank of doing this work really well was immense. A successful launch in China would be worth billions. The MD, Victoria McComb, wanted to dedicate some of her top people to the job, and to be rewarded accordingly. So she approached Excisient with a quote for the training services based on the value that would be created for the bank. The price was partly contingent on successful delivery of the project, and if fully successful would have worked out to about £240,000.

Excisient understood the logic of this value-based price, but insisted that the client would only pay for services on a day rate, and that the maximum rate available was £700 per day. Since McComb had been planning to spend only 80 days on the project, this would work out to no more than £56,000 – a tiny fraction of the value that the client would gain. At £700 a day it would be unprofitable to use their senior consultants on the project. Unable to persuade Excisient to raise the day rate or pay a lump-sum project fee, McComb was resigned to assigning junior staff to the project and doing a low-quality job.

Victoria McComb asked what the overall budget of the project was. Excisient gave a figure just over £1m, but indicated that the client was willing to throw vast quantities of resources at the project if necessary. This gave her an idea.

McComb realised that the total price of the project was not a barrier at all; the problem was merely a bureaucratic limit on the day rate paid to consultants. If they could spend more days on the project, and make it profitable, they could increase the total price and capture a fair share of the value the client would gain. She proposed a research exercise, in which McComb's student researchers would spend 300 person-days at £600 per day researching the Chinese market in endless detail, in order to create briefing reports for the trainers and the bank's staff. The trainers would do their job at £700 per day and the total project value would reach £236,000. The students would cost McComb a small fraction of the price being charged, and the extra profit would allow the firm to use its top people for the training.

Both Excisient and the bank were able to see that the value of the project would far exceed the price paid, and this structure helped bypass the day-rate limit that had been imposed in the procurement contract.

How to apply it

Revisit the benefit matrix you drew up in Chapter 1. For each of the benefits, work out the highest price that you could imagine anyone paying for that benefit.

Think about it in terms of the most expensive service or the most over-the-top luxury goods you can imagine. If the benefit is that the customer gets to look beautiful, imagine the most expensive haute couture dress or diamond-laden necklace you can think of. If the benefit is that your corporate client makes £5m in additional profits, imagine a financial deal in which they pay £4m to a bank to gain that £5m benefit.

These numbers may not be what you want to charge – because you may make more money by charging less – but they do at least provide a fair justification for a high price. If some customers are willing to pay £180,000 for a diamond necklace, then nobody should criticise you for charging £80,000 to provide the same basic benefit to another client.

When you have worked out the numbers for each benefit, add them all up. The total gives you a number you can use – if you need to – to justify your price.

Then look at your segmentation market research (Chapter 4) to see what evidence you have that people will really pay the price you want to charge. If the evidence doesn't suggest that they will pay it, you may in fact need to reduce your asking price, or go out and ask more questions to test the market again. Remember that people are led by your asking price. If you ask someone how much they'll pay for your product they will usually give a lower answer than their true willingness to pay. Imagine their answer is £5. The same person, if offered the product at £15, might well be willing to pay it. So to test accurately, you need to include the price point in your question, rather than expecting the consumer to tell you.

Finally, consider how much risk you are willing to take on the sale. Can you accept a return of the product if it doesn't sell at the price you claim? Can you prove the value that it will create, or make your price dependent on value?

Chapter summary

- People often have expectations about prices which are hard to change.

- Sometimes these are based on ideas of fairness, and sometimes on assumptions about what others are willing to pay for an item.

- Intermediaries, distributors and resellers think differently from consumers.

- To combat these attitudes and launch a product at your desired price point, you may need to both provide evidence and offer some kind of guarantee such as a sale-or-return deal.

Chapter 6

Memory and expectations, trials and reframing your prices

The alarm clock went off at 5.20am on 1 September. It had been a long time since I'd woken up this early. I dragged myself out of bed and got ready.

By 7am, I was outside a central London branch of Cosanostra Coffee. The doors opened and I went inside to watch and wait for the reaction of the first customers.

The promotional stand looked good – it highlighted the new product, allowed customers to sample the quality chocolate and smell the delicately flavoured tea leaves that went into each teapot. I chatted with the counter staff, who were intrigued by the new product. Both of them had tried it themselves during trials and were willing to recommend it to customers, even if they were not quite ready to abandon their morning espresso habit yet.

I bought one myself with a promotional voucher Maggie had given me, and settled into a table near the counter to listen for customer reactions.

On that first day, the notable feature was how little the price mattered. Customers were motivated by curiosity much more than cost. The prices were within the natural range for an espresso-based coffee (between £2 and £3) and this seemed to be accepted by those who were curious enough to try one out.

One thing that did make a difference was the refund promise. The branch I sat in during the morning offered money back for anyone who was not satisfied. I moved to a different branch in the afternoon which was not offering the same deal, and they had sold only half as many teapots. The perceived risk of trying the new product was substantially reduced by the reassurance that at least the customer's money was safe.

As I watched a few more branches over the next days, I noticed that some customers had examined the teapots on their first visit but did not buy until later. These people seemed to need to get used to the idea; and as one of them said: "It all looks very interesting, but I'm dying for an espresso." Moving people off their planned decision path while they are in the middle of purchasing is hard. Introducing a new option before they've made up their minds is much more likely to work. Some people on that second day would have set out with the intention of trying that strange teapot thing they saw yesterday; others will have seen it on promotion for three or four days before being willing to give it a try. New products require time to be integrated into the range of potential purchase options for a consumer – and for some products, and some people, they never will be.

The following week I visited a supermarket branch on the first day they stocked the teapots. Sales were not so quick here. A few people browsing for a smoothie or yoghurt did pick up and look at a packet of teapots, but it was an hour or two before anyone bought one. I managed to catch her on her way out of the shop and ask what had led to the purchase. It turned out she had tried one in a café and wanted to have some at home. So the strategy of introducing the product through the café channel seemed to be working.

Sales gradually picked up in the supermarkets over the next few weeks, but an unexpected pattern developed. Smaller teapots, priced at £1.59, were selling out, while the large ones at £1.99 were staying on the shelves. Maggie came into one of the stores with me one day to see how the customers were making their choices.

"We've been thinking of increasing the price on the small teapots to encourage people to buy more of the large ones," she explained. "The revenue isn't quite meeting the retailers' targets because too many people buy the small size. But we are not sure if we can put the price up without losing the customers we've already got."

"Isn't it worth losing a few of the current customers to get your revenue up?" I asked.

"In principle I wouldn't mind. But this might be a critical time. We are just starting to build our base of initial loyal customers and I'd hate to annoy them. But if we get stuck with this price point we are either going to lose money ourselves or lose orders from the supermarkets."

"So what are you going to do?"

A week later, I discovered Maggie's answer. Three new packages appeared on the supermarket shelves: a larger size teapot, a premium variation with single-estate Ecuadorian chocolate, and a white chocolate version. All of them were priced between £2.10 and £2.49. The original large teapot remained at £1.99, but stock levels were reduced.

After another week Maggie emailed me the sales results for the new products – a success! Revenue per customer had increased by 12%. The product had been successfully reframed, increasing revenue without hurting existing customers.

A product launch is a pivotal moment because it creates expectations in your customers' minds. Once established, these are hard to change.

Because it is hard to imagine and predict the future experience we will get from consuming a product, we must rely on our memories when we make a purchase. The memory of the last experience we had from a product or service is a complex and slippery thing, with many subtle attributes. The experience we will have when we next consume the product will be different on most of these dimensions. Is the weather different? Are we in a better or worse mood? More or less tired? But our memory of the price we paid last time is a single, simple number. It is much easier to compare today's price to last week's price than today's subjective product experience with last week's.

This makes it tough to change your prices. If the price today is higher than it was for the same product yesterday, this offers customers a clear reason (however insignificant the increase) not to buy. It is difficult for people to weigh up the relative importance of different reasons for a decision – but much easier to count the *number* of reasons for and against something. A price rise, tiny as it might be, is one reason against buying; a price cut, however small, is a reason to buy.

Therefore, no matter how clear your justification for a price rise – it may be a rise in the cost of ingredients, or the demand at the old price may be higher than you can cope with – it will hurt sales. You should look for ways to modify the presentation of your product so that customers do not do a straight price comparison between old and new. This is called **reframing** the decision.

A common method is to change the size of the package, or offer an extra product feature. Another technique is to increase the baseline price but offer a temporary discount. Sometimes the solution is to change price so often that customers lose their memory. Take a look at the price of a two-litre bottle of Pepsi or Diet Coke in your local supermarket over your next few visits. In the last two months, my local prices have shifted between £1.40 and £1.99, including variations such as two bottles for £2.99, a promotional discount from £1.89 to £1.50, and a variety of labelling strategies: in some cases a £1.79 promotional price printed on the label by the manufacturer, and in others a £1.99 price label affixed by the shop. On one occasion, the price even went both above and below this range at the same time – £2.06 for one bottle or £4 for four.

This inconsistency has the effect of blurring the consumer's memory of the standard price for the product. On those occasions when it is priced at £1.89, the buyer won't feel the instinctive antipathy they often experience towards a price increase. It may still feel like the bottle is at the expensive end of the typical range of prices, but the negative emotional reaction that would be provoked by 'the price has gone up' is greatly diluted.

Size reductions are commonly used as an effective price increase, though they have the drawback of not directly increasing revenue. However, a smaller pack can create 'space' in the range for you to launch a larger version later. Notice that many chocolate bars, which used to be sold in a single size, are now sold in a smaller standard size, plus a jumbo or 'king size' version which is more expensive. This method often does work, though you may have to accept some grumbling from clients who notice what you are doing.

How to apply it

Based on the benefit matrix developed in Chapter 1, you should have a number of different variables on which you can differentiate your product. Make sure you always keep some of these in reserve – for example the single-estate Ecuadorian version that Maggie held back instead of launching on day one. This will give you scope to introduce new price points without annoying customers who have got used to the existing prices.

You may want to launch some of these new variations with a temporary discount to encourage people to try them out. Your goal is to break their habit of buying the cheaper product, so that you can phase it out, increase its price or decrease its size without creating resistance or hostility.

Monitor your customers' reactions to the changes – not just when they are introduced but over time. The reaction will change over time, as they get used to the new strategies. Sometimes an initial price shock will put customers off, but they will return in time. Conversely, they might accept a change in price but as time goes on it will gradually prompt them to look elsewhere. A straight increase in price often has this effect: sales don't drop off immediately but over a couple of months they slowly decline. You can monitor this by continually speaking to customers, not just in the abstract, but – where possible – at the point of purchase. Ask them why they just bought – or didn't buy – your product. Ask them if they noticed its price.

The more price changes you make, the more data you will be able to gather about how customers respond to them. Not all customers will respond in the same way. If you are offering a business service to a small number of clients, it may be worth negotiating changes with them individually rather than applying a universal rule. If you are selling to consumers, you should make independent pricing decisions across different sales channels. (For most products, different sales channels, and therefore different buying behaviours, are more important than different demographics, so don't worry too much about separately asking the opinions of 55-year-olds and 25-year-olds.)

Where possible, keep open the option of reverting to previous prices, sizes or product options. Occasionally a change simply won't work, and you can often win back customers by switching back to a version of the product that they are already familiar with and in the habit of buying. If you plan the change correctly and manage it carefully, however, it is unlikely that you will need to reverse course.

Chapter summary

- Once a price precedent has been set, it is hard to increase.

- By temporarily varying prices downwards with a promotion, you will be able to raise them back to the original level afterwards.

- To increase overall prices you need to introduce new product variations or sizes.

In focus

Should you increase your prices in line with inflation?

Inflation drives pricing policy in several different ways. Your business's costs will increase over time. The purchasing power of a given amount of profit will decline. Your customers will have more money (in cash terms) over time. And, most importantly from a psychological point of view, customers expect prices to rise with inflation. This expectation is something you can use.

At the levels of inflation we have seen in the last 15 years – even the unusually high 5.4% rate that the UK reached in 2010 – the real effect of inflation on costs and incomes is likely to be drowned out by the specific changes in demand and costs for your particular products. If your product is energy-intensive, you will have seen big swings in costs as oil prices fluctuated between $50 and $150 per barrel. If your service involves software technology, the salaries of programmers have gone up a lot in recent years, but demand is likely to have jumped even more. Inflation has rarely been one of the biggest direct influences on business in this period (with the exception of fast-developing countries, especially China).

However, people still expect prices to go up every year. And this creates one of your only opportunities to adjust price outside of a new product launch.

In general, customers are suspicious of changes in price. They will notice a rise in price – however small – and if they have formed a habit of regularly buying your product, a price increase is one of the prompts that might lead them to reconsider their routine. A price cut, of course, is unlikely to have the same effect.

Increasing your prices due to inflation, however, is accepted as a fact of life. It commonly takes place in January, and aligns with the end of Christmas promotions or sales. Some companies impose a flat increase across the board based on the current published inflation rate. This at least lets them keep up with the average increase of costs and prices in the market, but it can be a wasted opportunity.

A better approach is to use the inflationary increase as a way to adjust relative prices within your product range. It is likely that you will have seen reduced demand for some products or services during the year, and increased demand for others. This is a chance to capture some of the increased demand in higher profits, by increasing the price of the high-demand items a bit more. For items which aren't doing so well, you might freeze or even cut prices. Customers are unlikely to work out the average increase overall, so there's no particular need to make sure this averages out to the precise inflation rate.

Make sure you promote the prices you have frozen – a phrase like 'Inflation buster' lets you point this out while implicitly explaining why the other prices have gone up. Customers who are very price sensitive may switch to the price-frozen products – while those who stay with their normal purchases are signalling a willingness to pay more (information that you can use in future promotions).

Should you do this in January with everyone else? You could keep your prices fixed in January and promote this fact, to show your customers that while their budget is under pressure everywhere else, at least they are getting a good deal from you. The problem is that when you get round to increasing them in June, you might be the only company doing so – and some customers may switch to your competitors. If your whole industry has adopted an annual price cycle outside January, it is probably best to align with that. A better approach may be that followed by the Pret A Manger sandwich chain, which changes several items in its product range every month, and can therefore impose an average price increase without anyone being able to tell. If an egg and roasted tomato sandwich costing £2.99 replaces a smoked mackerel baguette costing £3.50, is this an increase or a decrease? Only Pret's finance department knows.

These small individual decisions make a significant difference across the whole economy. Economists suggest that a little bit of inflation is a good thing because it allows companies to make adjustments to relative prices and wages which people would otherwise resist. For an economy to grow, it's important that prices and salaries adjust – so that products which are more valuable become relatively more expensive, and people who are more productive are paid relatively more – but this means conversely that people who are less productive or products less in demand must earn less money. Companies find it as difficult to cut salaries as they do to raise prices, but inflation does the job of automatically cutting wages by a few per cent each year; so companies can reduce the relative rewards for less productive people by simply not increasing the wage every year. In general, economies with inflation of 2%–5% a year are likely to be more flexible, and do better, than economies with either zero inflation or inflation in double figures.

Chapter 7
Anchoring

Sometimes a customer just doesn't know what your product is worth to them. We are used to thinking of this as a problem. If someone doesn't know the value of what you do, it feels as though they won't be willing to pay for it.

That's not necessarily so. We call this "unknown expected utility", and it gives you a superb opportunity to shape the customer's perception of what your product is worth. The primary method for doing that is called anchoring. I learned all about this on another visit to the teapot factory.

Maggie walked me downstairs to the factory shop. By this time the Chocolate Teapot Company was becoming well known, and every day a stream of tourists and fanatical customers visited for a tour. After seeing how the heatproofing technology is applied by the hand-built machines on the upper floor, and viewing the research labs in which new flavours of tea and chocolate are tested together, they ended up in the shop.

But there were two entrances to the shop, and Maggie showed me the difference between them. We watched some customers go in through the north entrance. The first thing they encountered was a display of smaller one-shot teapots for everyday use. Prices ranged from £1.30, for a single-layer milk chocolate pot, to £2.55, for a two-layered version with bitter cocoa overlaid on a rich vanilla white chocolate base. As we observed for a few minutes, we saw that, if they selected anything from this shelf, the majority of clients picked a cheaper pot.

We walked over to the south entrance, where another stream of customers was entering. These customers first saw a luxurious display of the high-end World Chocolate range, with specially selected cacao bean blends from a variety of locally owned African producers. Prices here were up to £6 for a single pot, or £25 for a gift box with a range of several different chocolate styles and flavours.

Most customers seemed intrigued by these products, but only a few of them picked one up off the shelf. However, when these customers subsequently stumbled upon the everyday display, their attitude seemed different. Having been exposed previously to the expensive range, they were much more interested in the £2.55 teapots than the cheaper £1.30 version.

On average, Maggie told me, those who entered by the south door were spending about 60% more than those who came in through the north entrance. In fact, the merchandising team planned to come in the next day and rearrange the store layout to replicate the more profitable presentation across both entrances.

Maggie introduced me to her head of merchandising, Julie Robinson, who explained her theory of how this process worked.

"When they enter this shop, most customers have no idea of the correct price for a chocolate teapot. Maybe 2p would be appropriate, given that that's about the price of a teabag. Or maybe £3.45, which is the price of a large cup of hot chocolate at Starbucks. There's a huge range of potential values. We'd argue that the daily experience of enjoying your favourite drink is worth several pounds to most people, and for an occasional indulgence you might easily spend £20 or more. But we don't have enough staff to walk round the store with each customer trying to persuade them of that. So we use pricing as a cue to value instead.

"First impressions are really important. When a customer is wondering about the worth of a teapot and the first price tag they see is £1.30, it sticks in their mind. Anything they subsequently see that's above that level looks like an expensive, luxury version. But when the first one they see costs £6, their subconscious assumption is that £6 is what people pay for this kind of thing. £2.55 looks reasonable, and £1.30 is downright

cheap. Too cheap, in fact, for some people – and so they tend to opt for a more expensive version.

"Whatever people think of as the default price, all others will be compared with it. Anything too cheap looks suspicious, while we have learned to indulge in more expensive products only occasionally. So the default price – which is called the anchor – sets the benchmark for what they're willing to pay."

Maggie interrupted. "I don't entirely agree. There's something else happening. Sure, there's something to the 'first impressions' idea, but I think we also change our minds when we see new prices. So a person who sees the £1.30 pot first, and then the £6 pot, is still willing to pay more than someone who has only seen the cheaper product.

"On some level – maybe not fully conscious – the customers are remembering all the prices they've seen for this type of product. Then when they look at a specific item, they compare it to the whole range. So this product type – one-shot teapots – has a £1.30–£6 range. And the £1.30 product is right at the bottom of a fairly wide range. Customers therefore draw the conclusion that it's not very good. And if they can trade up to a £1.50 or £2.50 product, they will feel much more comfortable that they're getting something of quality."

Research shows that Julie's idea that first impressions count and Maggie's theory that the range of prices matters are both valid. Academic experiments have found both effects to be true, and as the teapot merchandisers found, it's quite straightforward to use both of them at the same time.

The technical name of the 'first impressions' effect is **anchoring**, and it has been seen in dozens of economic lab experiments and countless commercial settings.

In an experiment with MIT undergraduates, Dan Ariely and colleagues auctioned off some tricky-to-value items – wireless keyboards, boxes of luxury chocolates and obscure French wines. The trick was this: before the auction, they asked each person to write down the last two digits of their social security number and ask themselves 'Would I pay this number of dollars for the item?' So someone with the social security number 440-84-8398 was looking at an initial price tag of $98, and their fellow student with the number 232-20-3911 started instead with $11.

These price tags were not part of the auction – it was a straightforward process where the highest bidder bought the product – but they had a huge effect on the bids that the students placed. Those with high digits ended up bidding about 50% more than those with low digits.

I have repeated a version of this experiment at many conferences and talks – and even when people are aware that I'm talking about pricing psychology, and many of them can guess exactly what I'm trying to prove, it still works. This effect is so strong that even when we consciously try to adjust for it, we usually can't.

Case study
Business consultancy

Consultancy businesses can use anchoring very effectively, for two reasons. First, consulting is a very non-commoditised business: it is difficult to compare one consultant with another, so clients are unlikely to have a clear pricing assumption already in their head. Second, you are often preparing a bespoke quote for each client, so you can create a range of solutions at very different price points with complete credibility. (The 'credibility' question is one which worries a number of businesses, so if you are concerned about this see Chapter 5).

So when you are asked for a quote by a client, offer at least three options:

- **A high-end, everything-including-the-kitchen-sink quotation**, which covers everything they could possibly want. I'll call this the A package, though you would probably want to choose a more expressive name such as 'in-depth support service' when you describe this option to your client. This might be priced, for example, at £60,000 for a project (the exact numbers will vary according to the situation, of course). You don't expect most clients to go for this size of project, but some might – especially bigger companies for whom the value of getting it right will far outweigh the cost of your service. However, what it does is establish that the value of what you offer **can** be at this level or above.

- **A middle-of-the-road option at, say, £19,000** – the B package. This is the level you think most clients should go for. The service should be clearly distinguished from the high-end option, so that clients who are considering the A package have good reasons to stay with it instead of trading down to the B package. But it should still include most of the key benefits of your service so that you don't risk losing the client to a competitor on the basis of a feature comparison. It's important that this option is not a hollowed-out version of your service – instead, the A package should have lots of luxury extras.

- **A cheap version at, say, £12,000** – the C package. It's OK for this one to be clearly inferior to the B package – it is meant to give people the option of spending less money but to feel that there is a good reason for them to move up to the standard B package.

Note the ratios in price: approximately 12:20:60 or 3:5:15. The numbers do not need to match these proportions exactly – a 1:2:4 ratio is also common – but these are good guidelines. The point is that the primary anchor, the A package, is significantly higher than your standard price; and that you still offer people at least two options even if the A package is too expensive for them. The C package is lower than the B package, but not too much lower. The overall effect of this structure is to set the expectation that some people are willing to pay the A price (so the product must be a high-value product) but that the real decision is between B and C, so B and C must be relatively close in price. If C is too low (say £3,000), it is more difficult for the customer to form a view on a core price band. So you should use B and C prices as an upper and lower boundary on what you want to portray as a sensible price.

(This approach also has the advantage of achieving successful **price discrimination**. See Chapter 3, 'Reading the customer's mind' to find out more about this.)

Downsides of anchoring

Standing outside the south entrance to the teapot store, I noticed a few customers approaching the shop and then wandering away without going in. When I pointed this out to Maggie, she nodded.

"People do seem to get the impression that this is an expensive store when they glance at the prices. The £6 and £25 packs are so prominent at this doorway that a few customers are put off going into the shop at all. We're not quite sure how much this matters. Those customers were probably never going to spend a lot. But we are trying something new soon – next time you're here come back and we'll take a look at how it's going."

You can find out the answer in Chapter 17, "Managing the pricing environment".

Anchoring has a powerful effect on the sales of the product you're focusing on, but it can have an effect on consumers' assumptions about your overall price levels. If you have high-priced anchor products it will be difficult to convincingly present an image as a discount or good-value supplier. In any case it is difficult to make those positions profitable unless you have very high volume and strong operational efficiencies, but some companies can do it. Most smaller businesses are better off with a high-value, high-margin positioning, and for these, anchoring is very powerful.

How to apply it

There are a lot of different ways to apply anchoring in most businesses. Here's a process you can follow to work out how best to use it.

1. **Collect data.** You want to know as much as possible about the range of prices that you and your competitors charge for a given product. Maggie had the advantage of a unique product for which no benchmark existed, but for most businesses, there are competitors or at least some kind of comparable product out there already (see Chapter 1 for more about this). Even if there are no direct competitors, find the range of things you'd like to be compared to – in this example, teabags and Starbucks mochas. Then compile a list of as many examples as possible, writing down the product name, who sells it, the size or quantity, and how much they charge.

2. **Order these by price level**, so that you can see the range of prices charged for similar products.

3. **Now consider the path a customer takes before choosing to buy your product.** Do they see a range of items in your shop? Or on your website? Or do they find different options by searching the Web? Is your product sitting in a shop alongside other similar products?

4. **Find where in that path you can add a new product at a high price.** If you are a retailer or if you sell products from your own website, you have a lot of control over this. You can place a high-priced option in front of the customer before they see your 'standard' product. If you have a product in someone else's shop, you have less direct control. But you can still try to persuade the retailer to display a higher-priced, luxury version of your product alongside the standard one (show them this chapter if you like – it is in their interest too!) or even try to place your product in retailers where the default prices are already higher (Waitrose instead of Sainsbury's).

5. **Choose your anchor price to be substantially higher than your standard price.** The anchor effect still works for a £5 product with a £6 anchor, but it isn't very strong. If two prices are close together, customers are likely to compare them directly instead of changing their subconscious evaluation of the true value of the product. But if you can put a £20 anchor alongside that £5 standard product, then the true value is much more likely to be shifted.

6. **If possible, try to measure consumer behaviour with and without the anchor.** There are at least three variables that can change: the number of consumers who buy anything at all; the proportion who buy this type of product; and the relative share of the £5 product versus other versions (for instance, if you have a £5 and a £3 version, which sells more?). Measurement is really important as there are lots of effects which may be going on at the same time, and you want to know which ones are stronger.

Collect data for anchoring

Product	Sold by	Quantity or size	Price
Hot chocolate	Starbucks	20oz (venti)	£3.45
Teabag	Tetley	1	2.5p
Teabags	Tetley	80	£1.99

Toolkit

You can copy this page and reuse it if you offer multiple products; or you can download more copies from www. psyprice.com.

Product	Sold by	Quantity or size	Price

Now design your product anchoring spectrum. Set the price of your core product to be close to whichever products from the above list you are competitively positioned against.

Product 1

Your core product	Cost price	Quantity or size	Price (a)

Your premium product	Cost price	Quantity or size	Price
			(a) + 100%

Your super-premium product	Cost price	Quantity or size	Price
			(a) + 200%

Product 2

Your core product	Cost price	Quantity or size	Price (a)

Your premium product	Cost price	Quantity or size	Price
			(a) + 100%

Your super-premium product	Cost price	Quantity or size	Price
			(a) + 200%

Product 3

Your core product	Cost price	Quantity or size	Price (a)

Your premium product	Cost price	Quantity or size	Price
			(a) + 100%

Your super-premium product	Cost price	Quantity or size	Price
			(a) + 200%

Product 4

Your core product	Cost price	Quantity or size	Price (a)

Your premium product	Cost price	Quantity or size	Price
			(a) + 100%

Your super-premium product	Cost price	Quantity or size	Price
			(a) + 200%

Chapter summary

■ Anchoring is one of the most powerful psychological effects relating to prices.

■ If you show someone a high price first, their expectations about the value of a product will be shifted upwards. When they then see the lower price which they will actually be charged, this will increase the attractiveness of your product or service.

■ People will compare the price of your product to the range of prices for comparable options. So if your price is £2,000 and the comparative range is £1,000–£10,000, you will look like good value. If the comparative range is £300–£2,000, you will look expensive.

Chapter 8

Competition

In January I went into the local Cosanostra Coffee for a chocolate teapot and spotted something I hadn't seen before: heavily promoted discounts on their regular menu of cappuccinos and Americanos. A whole range of key products – the medium size option on most drinks – were priced for the first time at 30p less than CTC's main price point of £2.89.

Was I tempted to switch? Not really. Thirty pence is quite a small temptation to switch product categories. But it did make me notice the offer. I decided to stay and watch for a while.

Over the next hour a stream of customers – maybe 50 or so – came into the shop. I'd watched this happen before, and there was a pattern: about half of the customers visibly notice the chocolate teapot shelf and eye it with curiosity. Of these, about one in five end up buying one to try.

This time, about the same number of people looked at the teapot display, but only a single person bought one. One sale instead of five – a serious impact on the number of people trying out the new product.

Later that week I mentioned this to Maggie.

"We spotted that. It's a bit of a problem for us. Our exclusive deal with that chain expired so they've lost some of their sales to their competitors. One of their people, name of Valerie Salmon, has just been promoted to head of coffee products and I think she wants to make her mark. She persuaded the head of retail that they need to make up the profit somewhere else.

Their espresso drinks are more profitable so they are promoting those instead. Existing customers are mostly staying with us, but new customers think the teapots look expensive compared to their regular coffee, and they aren't so keen to try it out. Sales from the café channel have stopped growing for the first time since we launched – they're exactly the same as last month."

"So what are you going to do?" I asked.

"I don't know yet. We tried to get them to offer a new promotion on teapots, but they wanted a 60% cut in our price to them. We can't offer that because we'd never persuade them to put the price back up again, even if we tried to make it a temporary offer. But it's critical to me that we get this chain back on board. Any ideas?"

I had none. I'd grown used to Maggie controlling everything about the pricing proposition, so it took me aback a little to hear her admit the next move was a mystery. My drive back to London was a thoughtful one.

Two days later, as I popped into a newsagent to buy that week's Economist, *I noticed a new magazine on the shelf.* Business Innovations *was a title I hadn't seen before – looking more closely, I discovered this was just the second issue – which appeared to focus on new and unusual business ideas and innovative companies.*

It was priced at £4.50, a little more than The Economist. *There was an interesting offer on the cover, though: a partnership with LinkedIn through which readers could be introduced to any two of the interviewees in the magazine. How unusual, I thought – and worth trying out.*

I wasn't expecting to have time to read two magazines this week so I ended up skipping The Economist, *though I ended up reading their "Economics Focus" and book reviews online as usual. So I bought* Business Innovations *and it turned out to be quite interesting.*

One of the articles was about a consultancy firm in London offering what was described as a revival of an old technique from the mail order industry. This firm was selling a new service to businesses – something to do with a newly invented marketing approach for websites – and they'd been having trouble getting people to try it out. Customers were being conservative: the firm believed in their service, but it was a newly developed technique which clients were a little wary of. Some prospective clients were pushing for price reductions as it was an untried technique; but the firm's owners did not want to reduce the perceived value of their service by cutting the price.

So they'd decided to offer a money-back guarantee on the first month of their service. The client could evaluate the service, decide whether it was giving them business value, and if it wasn't they could ask for a full refund.

Their sales had leapt about threefold. Sure, some clients did ask for their money back, but as a condition of the refund, the supplier insisted on detailed feedback and constructive criticism. This had helped to improve the service and, over time, the number of refund requests fell from 25% to only 10%. The money they lost on refunds was made up many times over by increased sales to clients who would never have tried the service otherwise.

I used one of my LinkedIn contacts to connect with one of the partners in the consultancy, Michael McGarry. Here's what he said:

"The guarantee makes a huge difference to our customers' perception of us. It takes away most of their perceived risk – when you tell them about the guarantee, they often don't believe you at first as it sounds too good to be true, but you reassure them and they generally come round to the question – where do I sign? In fact, it's enabled us to start turning away customers – we have developed a qualification process to see whether we believe they're serious enough about getting value out of our service. And there's an extra bonus: it shows clients that we believe in our own service, so they treat us with more respect and they seem more willing to believe in our advice."

Ultimately, he thinks, the money-back guarantee more than doubled the size of their business within a year and set it on course to grow significantly faster in the future.

My other contact was with Helen Sutherland, marketing manager of a business-to-business florist. Her interview in the magazine explained a different way of encouraging new customers to try their service.

"We realised that once a client has our flowers in their office every week, we have lots of ways to keep them loyal. We bring in special bouquets for birthdays and other events; we design flower arrangements in the corporate colours of our clients' customers, to help them impress those customers in turn; and we provide all sorts of extras to make sure their office environment is always improved by our being there, and that they'll miss us when we go. But before they've experienced us, they don't know how good we are.

"So we decided to offer a mini version of our service, just to make a little difference to a reception desk or entrance hall. We still charge for it – and it makes us a profit – but we use a longer-lasting pot plant, which is replaced just once a month, and deliver fresh herbs once a week to create a new aroma in the office. Some clients try it and then cancel after a couple of months; some stick with the mini service; but after a couple of months about 25% of them upgrade to the full service, which is where we make our real money."

Sutherland says that since adding the mini service, they are signing up about double the number of clients, though with many of them on the mini service, revenue has increased by only 40%.

Two weeks later I visited Maggie again. Her response to these stories was to set up a series of experiments in different branches of a different café chain.

In the first branch, CTC added a set of promotional offers to the teapots: competition entries or a voucher for a free biscuit. In the second, they tried a money-back guarantee – taste a chocolate teapot and if you don't like it, send us this voucher for a full refund. In the third, they introduced a miniature version of the teapot – more strongly flavoured and espresso-sized, at 99p.

Over the following weeks each of these offers increased the number of new customers recruited, by varying proportions depending on time of day and week. The promotional offers turned out to be the most effective of the three approaches.

In the next month CTC aggressively rolled out the promotion across all their Cosanostra branches. Sales leapt right away.

The café's total revenue went up, so the head of retail was happy. Reportedly, Salmon was not happy with the thwarting of her competitive approach, but with her boss on board she had no choice but to put up with it.

Competition has two faces. It can be a good thing – if you sell something very unusual, gaining a competitor is a powerful way to build credibility for your product category. You get to piggyback off their marketing, and the fact that there are two or more product choices gives customers confidence that other people are buying the product.

But it is also dangerous, because it creates the risk that people will look at your product purely on price. If your customers start to compare you on price with competitive alternatives, you may have to reduce your price to beat theirs. They will be forced to cut their price to beat you, and ultimately you will both end up getting cheaper and cheaper until you have no profit left.

To beat this, you need to distinguish your product from the competition so that customers can't easily compare your offering with theirs.

You might be able to do this by adding extra features to your product – though the competition may copy your features after a while. You can do it by using unusual package sizes so that customers have difficulty making a direct comparison – but you risk putting people off if they are used to buying the product in a specific size. And you can do it with specific offers, such as a money-back guarantee or extras such as a prize draw.

Dominant market share: low price

If you're aiming for the dominant position, you want to reduce the complexity for customers of comparing your product with the opposition. Try to match the format (for instance the 330ml can), the positioning and promotion (for instance try to get on the same shelf space in your retailers) and make clear what your advantages are without differentiating the product too much. Your goal is to take advantage of buyer inertia. People already in the habit of buying Innocent smoothies may consider your alternative product if it appears to be a close enough substitute and the price is lower.

The price differential you need to apply will depend on the strength of customer loyalty to the brand, and the significance of the purchase relative to the customer's disposable income. If you are selling a Coca-Cola competitor in newsagents in the City of London, it's unlikely that you will attract much switching unless your price is savagely lower – say 25p in comparison to the typical 69p retail price. On the other hand, if your goal is to sell a new flavour of fizzy drink to schoolchildren, the required differential will be smaller. In this case, the local newsagent will already be charging less – say 55p – and you will attract a significant number of switchers at 45p.

Perhaps you are competing against a brand without Coca-Cola's strength, such as Innocent smoothies, or one where the brand, though familiar, adds little value to the experience – think of Andrex toilet paper. In these markets, buying habits are much less ingrained and a smaller differential will be enough to tempt some people to change. To check this out, look at whether supermarkets have a successful own-brand line in the category. If they do, price competition has a good chance of working.

High margin: niche positioning

If, as is more common, you do not have the scale or capital to dominate the whole market, you are more likely to profit from a high-margin product with additional benefits.

In the case of the cola market, you can see examples such as Inca Kola or Jolt Cola, which are aimed at specific niches (organic/authentic, and high-caffeine geek respectively) and priced accordingly. In the retailers where you can buy Inca or Jolt, they are priced at least 50% higher than Coca-Cola and Pepsi.

The strategy is to pick one main benefit area where you can overwhelmingly exceed the quality of the competition, and aim for people who care a lot about that benefit. In the case of cola, there is a segment of people to whom organic food is important, and this is the niche for Inca.

You can sometimes use additional benefits. Many people in this market object to large corporations like Coca-Cola, seeing them as symbolic of a capitalist system that they don't like. Therefore Inca can use its independent image as an extra selling point: this benefit is highly compatible with the appeal of organic food. If the benefits are not compatible, there is a risk of 'motivational crowding' where the extra benefit is ignored, or makes it harder for the consumer to make a decision. If Inca Kola were to offer free tickets to Premiership football games with its drinks, this benefit might actually be counterproductive and reduce sales. It certainly wouldn't bring enough extra revenue to be worth the cost. In fact, Inca is now owned by Coca-Cola, though most consumers probably do not realise the connection.)

To calculate the price premium you will attach to your product, examine the strength of feeling that customers attach to your additional benefit. If your product is directly comparable to the competition, you are unlikely to achieve anything above 100% premium – and 50% is more likely. If you go too high, you are likely to break the comparison: a cola priced at £2.50 will not be perceived as an everyday thirst quencher, but might work as a health drink (see Purdey's) or a high-end energy drink. The markets for these categories are much smaller, however.

The psychological goal is to piggyback on existing demand – people who want to buy a can of Coca-Cola – while attracting them with the extra benefit to consider paying a little extra. Again, the degree to which you can achieve a price premium will depend on the share of disposable income this product represents. It's easier to sell a bottle of Purdey's in the City than in a school tuckshop.

This technique is especially powerful in service markets, where it is usually relatively easy to vary the service you provide without investing in launching a whole new manufacturing process. Services are in any case less competitive: as they are less tangible, it is harder for people to compare two suppliers directly and these markets tend to be less commoditised than those for physical products.

Combining the techniques

You can combine a mass-market and a high-margin strategy, but you will need to decide which is your primary approach.

If you choose the volume approach, you will be giving up margin from some customers who are willing to pay more. To capture more money from these customers, you can offer a higher-quality variation of your product (or indeed more than one variation). See the chapter on 'price discrimination' for more details and examples.

If your main focus is the high-margin product, you may want to test a cheaper high-volume version in case it catches the market's attention. You should be careful to distinguish this clearly from your main product so that it does not dilute the perceived value of that. Even if this does not take off, it might still introduce new customers to your brand who may later upgrade to higher-value purchases. Lindt have successfully followed this approach in the UK, launching a small truffle egg which is positioned against Cadbury's Creme Egg, introducing new customers to the more expensive boxed Lindt products.

Defence: when someone uses these techniques against you

If someone is positioning above you with a premium niche product (if you are Coca-Cola and they are Inca), you may not need to defend immediately – they can take only a small percentage of your market and there may be better things on which to spend your time and budget. If you do have a product development budget, you may want to develop your own premium offering: once they have tested that a market exists, you can use your brand and distribution power to launch your own version.

A competitive attack in the other direction is more serious. It is generally a bad idea to directly cut your prices in response to a competitive price cut. So refer to CTC's three strategies to work out the best response.

1. A **promotional offer** is a good way to add value to your product without a price cut. You are showing customers that it's worth sticking with your brand because you invest in creating extra value for them; and by using time-limited offers, you reduce the customer's temptation to try something new out of curiosity.

2. A **money-back guarantee** is appropriate if your own product is relatively new, and if you are still trying to get people to try it out. This was the case for CTC, and is a good way to respond if a more established competitor cuts prices to try to keep you out of their market.

3. A **miniature or restricted version** is a way to achieve a price point that competitors probably can't match, without seriously damaging your margins or destroying the perceived value of your main product. In consumer

products, this can be a smaller pack size; in services or software, it might be a simpler or less customised service; or even a deliberately limited offering with features removed (common in the software market).

How to apply it

Applying these defensive techniques in your own business can be fun. To do so, look at your competitor comparison charts and work out the reasons why people might choose their product over yours. See what you can offer that will counter those reasons – something tempting enough to get them to switch to you without cutting your core price.

Developing a competitor comparison chart

In Chapter 1, you created a list of key product benefits and identified the competitive products that you wanted to position yourself against. Now it's time to look at the competition in more detail. For each of your product categories, pick two or three of the closest direct competitor products. Here's an example:

	Your product 330ml Super Cola	Competitor 1 330ml Coke can	Competitor 2 330ml Pepsi can
Their price points		45p–65p	42p–65p
Competitive advantage	Novelty	Strong brand Traditional image	Good brand Youthful image

Fill out one of the following blank templates for your own products, or download more at www.psyprice.com.

	Your product	Competitor 1	Competitor 2
Their price points			
Competitive advantage			

	Your product	Competitor 1	Competitor 2
Their price points			
Competitive advantage			

You now have a decision to make. Do you have the marketing budget to aim for a dominant market share? And is this the position you want? If so, you need to be competitive on price but also offer some other advantages.

Or do you prefer to be a high-value, high-margin supplier with a niche position? If so, you should deliberately pitch your prices above those of the competitors and make sure that – within your niche – you have a series of product advantages so overwhelming that your competition can't touch you.

It is possible to achieve premium price and dominant market share at the same time, but it's very hard to do, and if you aren't the first into a market, you need to start with one of the other two strategies. However, you can achieve both quality and price positioning with a stratified pricing structure – as outlined under 'Combining the techniques' above.

Chapter summary

- When there is already a product in the marketplace with which you can with compete, you can get a shortcut to consumer acceptance by positioning your product as a better or cheaper version of theirs.

- Customers will find it easier to compare your product with a competitor than to evaluate it on its own merits. Work out every way in which they could be compared, and try to make your product better on the majority of them.

- Of course, competitors can do the same to you. Competition is more dangerous when the competitor's product is very similar to yours.

- If possible, avoid a straight price cut in response to competition. This creates a race to the bottom in which nobody can make any profit.

- The ideal strategy against a competitor is a 'squeeze', where you introduce two products – one slightly better quality and more expensive, and one slightly cheaper, than the competitor's product.

In focus
Pricing publicity

Every so often a pricing story hits the news. Usually this is for one of two reasons.

The good reason is that you've designed a clever pricing approach which may revolutionise your industry. Low-cost airlines were a big story in the 1990s, and everyone from estate agents to iTunes have made hay out of new pricing schemes, especially those that are clearly better both for customers and for the company.

The bad reason is when you are being portrayed as overcharging. Fortunately for most of us, there is so much overcharging out there that only the biggest companies are likely to be written about. Prominent examples included the following.

- Airlines being accused of adding on excessive fees and charges to their advertised price.

- Mobile phone companies billing £30,000 for data roaming.

- Bank of America's $5 per month fee for using a debit card.

- Verizon settling lawsuits for millions of dollars for overcharging and rounding up data charges.

- Orange unilaterally increasing its phone subscription charges halfway through a contract.

- UK electricity companies regularly being accused of increasing prices when the oil price goes up, and not cutting them when it falls.

Whether or not these accusations are based in truth, whether they are fair or not, the publicity is damaging. Social media in particular offers a new channel for customers to communicate and organise a campaign against a company. Bank of America backed down from its plans to charge that $5 fee after extensive protests on Twitter and Facebook.

If you're a small company, the chances of a campaign like this are correspondingly small. People tend to assume that big corporations have market power, while it's easier to walk away from a small firm if you're not happy. Still, it's worth being aware of what kind of pricing is likely to lead to objections.

Charging for something that has previously been free is one risk. So is charging one set of customers who were previously cross-subsidised by another. Bank of America made both of these mistakes: the transaction fees they earned from retailers were capped by a new law, so they tried to make up the money by charging account holders instead. Airlines that started to charge large fees for debit card use opened themselves up to the same complaint.

Charges with no convincing basis in cost are sometimes open to attack. Those airlines again: charging one transaction fee for a debit card payment was perhaps justifiable, but to charge £5 each way for each passenger in a single transaction – £40 for a return trip for a family of four – was hard to stand behind.

Offsetting one charge with another is often a good defence – low-cost airlines can argue that their charges are a reason why the base ticket cost is so low. Keep an eye on the net effect, though. If you have to cut one charge by more than the amount you make up on the other, there's little point.

Increasing the amount of an existing price, by contrast, rarely provokes much protest. Most consumers share a general assumption that companies should be allowed to charge what they want – the objections are often to the charging *model* rather than the total amount.

Sometimes the issue is genuinely out of your control. Energy companies in the UK can make a good argument that their high prices are a direct result of oil and gas prices; their profits at time of writing are only around 9% of sales, which doesn't seem unreasonable on the face of it. However, they could undoubtedly do a better job of reframing their price structures to reduce consumer resistance.

Of course, you might choose to ride out the objections. Netflix recently provoked a storm of protest by splitting its $10/month combined DVD + online streaming subscription into two separate $8 subscriptions. But they lost only 3% of subscribers in return for a 30%–50% increase in revenue. Ryanair has revelled for years in its harsh image, which combines ruthless cost-cutting and ruthless charging for anything beyond the basic service.

And some pricing objections are so irrelevant that they don't matter to normal customers at all. When a restaurant announces a £13,000 gold-plated truffle-and-foie-gras hamburger, it will probably neither gain nor lose any customers within the admittedly specialised truffle-and-foie-gras hamburger niche. But it might attract a few who will pay £75 for a steak based on the hamburger's publicity.

A general principle is: if your company is famous enough that its pricing becomes a news story, you already have a big advantage. If your company *gets* famous through its pricing initiatives, then no matter whether customers like your prices or not, at least you're famous now.

Chapter 9

Decoys

Asymmetric dominance: the bowler hat theory

Maybe it's worth mentioning where I first met Maggie.

My friend Keith decided two years ago finally to join the world of digital photography. On the basis of recommendations from friends (not me – I know better than to risk getting blamed for somebody else's purchase) he narrowed down the options to two cameras: the Sony Cybershot and the Nikon P510.

I went with him to buy one at the local camera shop, owned by a couple who seemed to have been there forever. Both models were there on the shelf. The Sony is light, small and easy to use. The Nikon has a longer battery life and a better-quality optical zoom. Here they are:

- *Nikon – 10 hours' battery life, 20x optical zoom, 600g, 5cm thick: £329*

- *Sony – 5 hours' battery life, 16x zoom, 350g, 2cm thick: £284.99*

Each has strengths and weaknesses, and Keith really wasn't sure which one he wanted.

The owners' daughter was working in the shop that day, on a break from her university course. As she came over to help us. I glanced at her name badge – Maggie.

After talking over the options with Keith and understanding his criteria for choosing between the products, Maggie asked him to wait a moment. She disappeared into the stockroom for a moment and brought out a bowler hat with a price label on it: £335.30. She placed the hat on the shelf next to the cameras.

Keith looked at this extra option for a while and decided to buy the Nikon. He thanked Maggie for her help and left the shop. Maggie, satisfied with her work, returned the hat to the back room and awaited her next indecisive client. I heard a few months later that the shop's landlord, a company called CLH Property, had refused to renew their lease – forcing the shop to close after 25 years. So they never had the chance to scale up Maggie's psychological pricing methods to a bigger scale.

Bizarre story, don't you think? The store offers a completely irrelevant product which the customer doesn't want – and is too expensive anyway – but it influences him to buy the product the shop wants him to. How could that possibly work?

Well, I have a confession. I've changed one little detail, but apart from this, the story is true.

In fact, the irrelevant product is not a bowler hat but another camera. It's another Nikon camera – last year's model, the P500. The battery life is only nine hours and the zoom 18x. And it costs £339.

Diagram 4

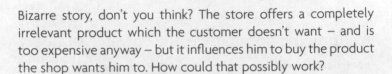

Camera comparison

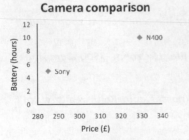

Decision 1. Comparing the different brands is hard. The Sony is cheaper, but the N400 has more battery life. Neithr is clearly better than the other.

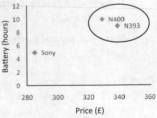

Decision 2. First compare the two Nikons. The N400 is clearly better than the N393 (or the bowler hat!) – both on price and battery life. The N393 acts as a 'decoy' and people subconsciously assume that the N400 is better than the Sony too.

Clearly nobody would buy the P500. It has no advantages over the P510, and it's more expensive too. Just like the bowler hat.

And yet it really does influence people to choose the other Nikon in preference to the Sony.

The reason? People find it hard to compare two products which have different advantages or different attributes. It's tough to know whether a more compact, lighter camera will be preferable in more situations to a higher-quality one with longer battery life. But it's very easy to compare it to a product with similar, slightly inferior attributes. Thus the P510 is definitely better than the P500. But the Sony is not clearly better (or worse) than either the P500 or the P510. So out of the three products, the P510 is the only one that's clearly better than any of the others. This is enough to make people choose the P510.

As we can see from the bowler hat example, this behaviour is not really logical – but many experiments have shown that it does happen, consistently. Technically, the effect is called **asymmetric dominance** and it happens whenever two products (A and B) are each superior to the other on a single dimension. For example, one may be better on quality and the other on price.

By introducing a third product, C, which is clearly inferior to B (on both dimensions), you make your consumers more likely to buy B than A.

And the simplest way to introduce an inferior product is to make it more expensive. So any time you have two products which compete on quality and price, and you'd like people to buy the more expensive one, simply add a third which is even more expensive, but no better in quality.

Case study

Decoys on services

The decoy technique applies just as well to services as it does to products.

A midsize law firm, Smith & Bloggs LLP, has a private client department that handles personal legal and tax matters for reasonably wealthy customers. One of the services it offers is drawing up wills for its clients. This is an in-depth, high-quality service in which it works out all the tax advantages of different trust structures, makes the appropriate recommendation to the client, and draws up the full documentation of the will, ensuring that all the implications are understood by the client and that they have the option to assign appropriate legal powers to a spouse or child. The will-writing service typically costs around £900 (with further set-up costs if a trust is established).

A local high-street firm that competes with Smith & Bloggs takes a simpler approach, without exploring the tax implications of the will, and charges only £400.

The critical benefit dimensions here are (1) tax savings and (2) price. How should Smith & Bloggs design a decoy service to attract more clients from its competitor? The answer is to offer a second will-writing service with smaller tax savings, but at a higher price. This might be a 'will for corporate assets, without trusts' service at £1,100. It would exclude the detailed tax and trust analysis but would allow the client to incorporate distribution of company assets in the will. This service is provided not by the original solicitor with all their tax expertise, but by a corporate lawyer with less experience in personal tax strategies. The extra expense comes from the fact that the corporate lawyer's chargeout rate is higher, and they are less experienced at preparing wills. For most clients, who do not have corporate matters to handle, this service will be inferior to the standard will-writing service. Very few clients will buy the corporate service, but it will increase the number of people buying the standard service at the expense of the high-street competitor.

Price-level decoys

As we saw in Chapter 1, people are often bad at estimating the value and benefits of a product. This is especially true when the specific product is unfamiliar (for instance many wines) or highly complex (mobile phone contracts or many business-to-business consulting services). In these cases, customers often use the price itself as a way to estimate value.

Would you expect a £40 bottle of wine to be better than a £7 bottle? Most people do. In fact, experiments show that consumers in a taste test usually say that a £40 wine tastes better than a £7 wine, even when it's actually the same wine with two different labels.

One group of researchers went a step further, in case the consumers were just *saying* that the £40 wine tasted better because they didn't want to look like they don't appreciate posh wine. So they put the consumers into an fMRI brain scanner and tested how their brain reacted to the wines. Even though the two wines were exactly the same, the consumers showed greater activity in those parts of the brain related to sensing pleasure when they believed it was more expensive.

In cases like this, price and value are collapsed into a single dimension. It's not possible then to use the asymmetric dominance style of decoy described above.

Instead, a decoy can be created through price alone. Let's see how that can work.

After buying his new camera, Keith walked into the bar next door to relax with a glass of wine. On the menu were two white wines by the glass: a French vin de pays at £3.45 and an Italian pinot grigio at £4.15.

Keith was about to order a glass of the £3.45 wine. Like most people, he is more likely to choose the cheaper product when he has little information to guide him. In our experiments, around 70% of people will choose the lower-priced wine from two options.

As he was about to order, the bartender blatantly ignored him and turned to another customer who, Keith was sure, had not been waiting as long. Annoyed, he decided he didn't like the music in that place anyway and decided to go around the corner to a quieter pub. In this one, the menu was slightly different.

- French vin de pays: £3.45

- Italian pinot grigio: £4.15

- New Zealand sauvignon blanc: £5.20

The only difference: the addition of one, more expensive, option to the menu. This option wasn't particularly of interest to him – it was quite expensive, and, like most people, Keith was not confident that he would appreciate the difference in taste of a higher-end wine.

But in this pub, Keith, still a typical consumer, ended up choosing the pinot grigio – not the cheapest but the middle-priced wine. He spent 80p more, increasing the pub's profits by about 60p. Why does this happen? The way he makes his decision this time is similar to the cameras, but a little different.

The key effect is that we don't like to pick extreme options – we like compromise and balance, because it feels that way we are less likely to make a mistake. This is sometimes called the 'Goldilocks effect' after the girl who chose porridge which was not too hot or too cold, but just right. When there are only two options, as in the first bar, both choices are extreme. One is the highest and the other is the lowest option, so people can't use this as a criterion. When there are three, the middle option becomes very attractive regardless of its intrinsic benefits.

The other explanation for this – and both reasons are true to some extent – is called **diminishing marginal utility**. This essentially means that the taste difference between the best and second-best wine is smaller than the difference between the second and third. But the price difference is just as great, or in this example greater. Thus, when Keith compares the two cheaper wines he's quite likely to want to upgrade to the higher of the two. When he goes on to compare with the most expensive, he's less likely to want to upgrade a second time. This effect, combined with the anchoring phenomenon explained in Chapter 7, explains the effectiveness of the third option.

Years later, when I saw the variety of extra teapots being launched in the supermarket chain particularly − with their different flavours, sizes and chocolate quality − I recognised the same decoy effects at work. I was never quite sure which of the teapots were the decoys and which were the real products, but total sales were consistently higher in the stores that stocked the decoys than in those that decided not to.

How to apply it

There are two different approaches to implementing decoys in your business. The first is the **asymmetric dominance approach**, as used in the camera example in this chapter.

The analysis of values and benefits you did in Chapter 1 revealed the critical value dimensions of your product or service. For a tangible product like a camera, these dimensions may be features such as zoom level or battery life. For intangible services the dimensions may be the years of experience and expertise you have as a lawyer, and the insurance you carry to protect your clients from risk.

Look at the buying situation, where the customer is comparing your product or service with those sold by a competitor. Work out on which value dimensions (or benefits) your offering is better than theirs, and on which dimensions theirs is better. If your product is better in every dimension, the customer would already have bought it! So the competition must have some kind of advantage, even if it is only a cheaper price, or a more familiar brand.

Let's say that your product has a longer battery life (eight hours versus five), but theirs has a better zoom level (18x versus 16x). This gives people a genuine reason to stop and think: which product they choose depends on them trying to figure out whether battery life is more important than zoom. Now you invent a new decoy product which is dominated by your original product. In this case, the decoy has a slightly shorter battery life (seven hours) than your original product, and is about 3% more expensive. Clearly nobody will want to buy that one. But adding it to the shelf will make your real product more attractive.

The general principle is to introduce a second product which is slightly inferior to your main product in all (or most) of the benefits. This will distract the customer from the competitor's product.

Price-level decoys are a simpler technique to implement. Whatever your service, simply look at the options you are offering to a typical client. If you offer three options already – as long as they have different price points – you don't need to do anything. You are already implicitly offering a decoy.

If you offer only two products, simply add a third, premium option which is priced well above the higher of the two existing choices. If your two options are priced at £800 and £1,300, take the difference (£500), add 20% to get £600, and add that to the higher price to work out the price of the new premium option, £1,900. It doesn't matter too much how you design the premium product: it could be an extra high-quality version; it could include extra services or upgraded features. The one thing not recommended is to increase the quantity or volume of the product – this runs the risk of making the new product look like a cheap 'family pack' rather than a premium choice.

Finally, if you currently offer just one product, you need to add two options. The two options should both be more expensive than the current one. The exact proportions depend on the competitive dynamics and how people value your services, but a good rule of thumb is 3:4:6. That is, if your service costs £6,000, add a third to get the price of the middle option – £8,000 – and another 50% to get the price of the top product – £12,000. Compare this with the price ratios recommended in Chapter 7 ('Anchoring'), which cover a wider range. Decoys are more likely to be of use when customers have some expectation of the existing market price point for the product. The wider price ranges are effective when you are defining a new segment or new product type – you want to match the biggest possible range of different valuations that different customers might place on the product.

Case study

Self-decoying

This magazine publisher has no direct competitors in its market, but has two of its own product options. It sells subscriptions to its weekly magazine in two different formats: a print subscription at £120/year and an online version at £75/year. It would much prefer people to opt for the printed version – there is more profit in it, and it gets much better advertising rates – but it still needs to offer the online version for those who are highly price-sensitive and to build its search-engine rankings.

How can it influence people towards the print version? In this case the printed magazine is more tangible and easier to read, but the online version is cheaper and available more quickly. So its decoy would be a slightly worse version of the printed edition: for instance, a printed version delivered monthly in a presentation binder instead of weekly, and sold for £135. Most subscribers do not want to wait a month for their magazine, nor will they pay more just for a binder, so this option is strictly inferior to the print product. It will, however, work as a decoy. It is likely that around 10% more customers, when offered all three options, will buy the print edition rather than the online subscription.

The cost of offering decoy products

The question arises: should you actually manufacture the decoy product or is it just a fictional offering to distract customers? The risk you face is that someone actually orders it.

In most service businesses, it will be easy to offer a variation on your main offering because you are carrying out each service on request; and in product businesses where there are older, inferior versions of products, you can use old stock as the decoy. In others (such as the magazine binder example above) you may be able to have the decoy product manufactured on demand in the rare cases when someone orders one. But in some businesses, it can be expensive to produce a new product, especially when you are not expecting to make enough sales of it to pay back the startup costs. If this is the case, you may find it better to modify one of the products you already have, perhaps by removing or disabling a feature. The idea of a decoy is that it should be sufficiently similar to your main product that it is easy both for consumers to compare and for you to produce without much extra cost.

If you really can't think of another way to offer a new variation on the product, just take the same product, give it a new name and offer it at a higher price. This will work perfectly as a decoy, as it is, in the economic jargon, strictly dominated by the real, slightly cheaper product.

In any case, few consumers will order the decoy product. In theory, nobody should ever want it, so if someone mistakenly asks for one you may be able to get in touch with them and suggest they take the real, non-decoy version instead. You'll be doing them a favour.

Chapter summary

- Customers instinctively want to make comparisons between products. This makes their buying decisions easier.

- Therefore you want to give them options which are definitively worse than your main product.

- If you can introduce these 'decoys' into the buying process, you will make your product look subconsciously better than it would without the decoys.

- If it is hard for people to compare the features or quality attributes of two products because they are not numeric quantities, you can use the price of the product itself as a decoy.

Chapter 10
Paying tomorrow for what you get today

I thought at first it was just selective attention. You know how once you've booked your holiday to Tunisia you suddenly see the adverts for it everywhere? Well, I saw a lot of chocolate teapots that April, but I figured my senses were just on high alert.

I mentioned it to Maggie on my next visit, but she thought otherwise. "It's not an illusion – it's real. We're selling about three times as many as last month – and I can show you why."

You can imagine my intrigue, but Maggie didn't want to tell me right away. We got into her car and she drove me to the local supermarket.

We headed for the coffee and tea aisle and there, as usual, was a shelf of chocolate teapots, with the usual range of different flavours and sizes, a few of which I hadn't seen before. Hanging from the handle of each one was a promotional label: Drink today for free.

Maggie was visibly excited by this. "This is one of our best ideas so far. We struck a deal with the mobile phone operators and now you can get your teapot on instant credit. Try it."

I took a teapot from the shelf and brought it to the supermarket counter. The cashier scanned the promotional label and asked whether I wanted to pay now or next month. Prompted by Maggie, I said next month would be better for me. She then asked me to fill in my mobile number on the label – typed it into her till – and moments later, I received a text containing the code 44939. She asked to see it, typed it into the till and I walked off with my teapot.

"It's even better if you go into Caffe Milano," Maggie said. "You can text them before you get there and they'll have the teapot ready-boiled for you to take away. The number of impulse purchases we've had has gone up by about eight times."

"So how is this different from just putting it on your credit card?" I asked.

"This is a completely different psychological process. Human beings are trained to be sensitive to the pain of paying money out of our pocket. This means that even when a process involves only metaphorical money – like a credit card or a storecard – some of the pain effect still carries over. However, when the cost is instead absorbed into a place where you are relatively insensitive to small changes in value – your monthly phone bill – the pain goes away."

I thought about it. It certainly had felt – sort of – like getting a free teapot. Though I had the concern that I would be paying for it eventually, and I wasn't sure how I would feel once the bill came through.

Maggie continued. "It's not just the pain issue. It takes away a barrier to purchase: having no cash in your pocket. How often have you checked your pockets before going into a café and then turned away – or bought something different from what you wanted – because you were short of change? It happens a lot, especially among younger people. Even those who do have enough cash on them are tempted to spend more – our proportion of premium teapots has gone up by about 10 percentage points among phone-pay users."

Opening up my teapot to drink it, I noticed another offer on the packet: Make sure you get your daily teapot every morning in time for breakfast. *This one I hadn't spotted before. The offer: for £1.92 a day, I could have my teapot waiting for me at Caffe Milano each morning the minute I arrived; or for 99p a day the teapots would be delivered to my home ready for me to add hot water.*

"Do people actually sign up for this?" I asked Maggie.

"About 8,000 so far," she said. "It's a simple subscription plan – we charge them on a monthly direct debit and they get the teapots delivered. They get a cheap deal, we get guaranteed custom, for a while at least. Everyone's happy except the competition. Cosanostra Cafe is trying to say we're competing unfairly with them and we should stop the scheme. But you know when someone's complaining that much you must be doing something right."

"Are people really so keen to buy things on credit? Even after the recession? I thought everyone was paying off their debts, not taking on new ones."

"They are: at least, they're paying off what they think of as debts – bank loans and credit cards. Fortunately for us, these are not really debts in a substantive sense – the payment is always taken within 60 days – and the customer doesn't seem to think of them that way."

"And you aren't worried that you're encouraging people to spend what they can't afford?" I asked.

"Well, we hardly get any non-payment of the bills – maybe about 2%, which is easy to absorb in our profit margins given the extra volume it generates. And I think people have to decide for themselves what they can afford. Our product isn't addictive, so we have to assume the customer is capable of making a correct decision. They can always stop buying it if they want to, but so far only one in 10 has cancelled their subscription."

Back in the office, I looked up the research behind this idea.

Both concepts, it turns out, are a variation on **hyperbolic discounting**. This phenomenon, discovered by psychologists in the 1960s and examined in economics research in the 1980s, says that people put much less value on money in the future than in the present. Of course this is part of how we all manage our finances – £100 this month is worth about £105 this time next year, if interest rates are 5%. But when you bring the payment forward right into the present moment – as most retail purchases do – the effect is much stronger than that.

Essentially there is a resistance to spending money – and a corresponding desire to gain money – in the present moment, which is much stronger than the normal interest rate effect.

If Maggie offers me £100 next week, or £110 in two weeks, I will almost certainly prefer the £110 in two weeks. It's 10% more and I only have to wait an extra week to get it – that's quite logical. I quite rightly believe that 10% is a very generous interest rate for waiting a whole week.

But if she offers me a choice between £100 *right now* and £110 in *one* week, my decision changes. Suddenly 10% doesn't seem such a good compensation for waiting a week. The impulse of getting money now versus the uncertainty of what might happen between now and then makes me more likely to choose the £100 today.

The exact amounts, the lengths of time and the interest rates all vary. But this technique works effectively across many different consumer products and industries. It's all about deferring payment while offering the benefit of the product today.

Furniture shops are famous for this. Not only do they win customers who would otherwise not buy at all with their interest-free credit deals, but they get people to spend a lot more than they otherwise would. There's even some rational logic to this – I get the benefit of a sofa over its lifetime, so why not pay for it over at least part of that timescale? But the effect isn't really about rationality. It's about deferring the pain of payment. For £899 out of my pocket, I can probably live with the old sofa for a bit longer. But for £38 a month over three years – with the payments not even starting for two months – why not indulge in a bit of luxury now? After all, it's been a hard week and I'd just love to sink into that new sofa with its fresh smell while I load up a DVD and a glass of wine.

As Maggie showed, this can be applied to any industry, for example if you sell a service to small businesses. Many of them are always short of cash – and may indeed be into their overdraft. Offering payment terms or credit is a good way to get people to buy now despite their uncertainty about paying next month's wages.

If you sell to consumers, any way you can get them to commit to buying a high volume without having to pay for it up front is likely to increase volumes and reduce price sensitivity.

Another effect contributes to this: the idea of **psychological distance**. Psychological distance applies to any object, or decision, or experience that you think of in a way displaced from your current experience. This distance could be in time, if you are thinking of something that will happen in the future. It could be in space, if you think of something that is happening far away. Or it could be conceptual distance – an experience that is more abstract or vague, less concrete. All of these kinds of distance make the idea of payment less tangible, while the benefits do not diminish correspondingly. The cost–benefit tradeoff is changed, and people become willing to pay a higher cost for the same benefit.

There are risks to delayed payment, of course: some clients may fail to pay the bill, or at least part of it, and others may cancel their subscription soon after taking it out. Depending on the details of what you do, you may legally have to offer a cooling-off period of a week or two (allowing people to cancel the payment plan if they change their minds – though of course in this case they must also return the product). For certain things you might also need a consumer credit licence, though this would be unusual if you sell to businesses. Worth checking with a lawyer – and don't let them make you pay up front!

All these costs are probably worthwhile, though. Experiments and informal experience indicate that some consumers will pay up to 50% more for a product if they can pay for it later rather than handing over the cash now. That's a huge extra margin you can access with a simple change of timing.

How to apply it

Consider the time period over which your customers will use your product.

If you have a one-off purchase, if the consumer buys and uses your product immediately, then it is hard to use this technique. But if they are buying it to use in the future, or if they are going to make repeat purchases, or if they are buying something whose benefits they will experience over a long period, then you have a good opportunity to use this approach.

Draw a chart like this, graphing benefit received from your product against time.

Diagram 5

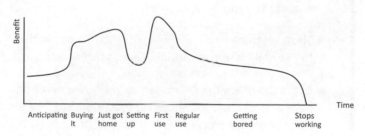

Mark the horizontal axis according to an appropriate time period and highlight the key benefits or values of your product on the vertical axis. Many products will have an initial period of high value, followed by a gradual slow decline of value over time. Imagine when you first get a new car, or move into a house – you will have a surge of pleasure and novelty over the first weeks or months, and once you get used to it this will decline. After a while the value becomes fairly steady, though over a long period the value reduces as the car or house becomes older – the bumpers get scratched or the boiler starts to make funny noises when it starts up.

Work out how you can link what the customer pays to the benefit they get. And once the value declines below a certain level, think about how you can offer them something new – a new car, an extension to the house, or a different flavour of tea – to restore that surge of initial value they once had, and get them to pay you again.

Chapter summary

- Customers experience the act of paying for something almost as if it is a physical pain.

- The experience of pain in the present moment is far more sharp and intense than pain in the future, which is easier to rationalise or ignore.

- Thus, anything which allows customers to pay in the future will make them more likely to buy now.

- If it is too much trouble to set up your own deferred payment scheme, you should at least try to accept payment by credit card, which achieves the same goal but lets the credit card company worry about making sure the customer pays up.

In focus

Negotiating

Most of the advice and examples in the book are structured around the pricing of standard products or services – a teapot, a haircut or a piece of jewellery. But many businesses don't sell standard products. If you work in a consultancy, or in most professional firms, or indeed in any kind of service, there's a good chance that you prepare a custom proposal and quote for any client, and then negotiate from there to reach a final price.

It turns out that you can use most of the same principles in this context. Positioning is still important – working out the values of the client and deciding how to pitch your service. You can do this even more accurately when you know the concerns and wishes of the specific client.

Price differentiation and anchoring work too. A good way to do this is usually to offer the client several different services, starting with a very expensive option, and then gradually scaling down to a more limited version. A management consulting firm might start out by offering the client a project costing £1.5m plus 2% of client revenues over three years, and then offer a set of more cost-effective or lower-risk options at £300,000, £100,000 or £40,000. As long as the services are clearly distinguished from each other, this encourages the client to reveal how big a budget they are willing to spend by selecting the option that fits best. (If you can get them to tell you their budget in advance, that's usually even better, but be aware this risks getting the client mentally anchored to a figure, where you might otherwise have a chance to influence them to go higher.)

You can use hyperbolic discounting and decoys in the same way as with a standard product, as well as social effects by discussing what other clients are already paying. You can also research what the competition is likely to do and respond accordingly.

The main challenge is the time it takes to draw up a customised quote. Fully analysing the situation and deciding which pricing techniques to apply could take a few hours, days or even weeks. You may want to draw up one formula that you can apply in many different situations. An example might look like this:

Estimate the number of hours required for the service, and your standard hourly rate	Standard option	100 hrs × £120/hr = £12,000
Add 60% to the hours and 30% to the rate for a 'high-service' option: the client will receive personal attention from a senior person, extra project management and other additional services	Premium option	160 hrs × £156/hr = £24,960
Add 30% to the hours and 20% to the rate for a middle option	Advanced option	130 hrs × £144/hr = £18,720
Offer a subscription option: divide the Standard Option price by 15 to give a monthly price over two years; this includes standard service plus some followup meetings and additional support	Subscription option	£800/month over two years
Offer a value-pricing option which ties your rewards to the number of new customers they win, or the productivity saving they make, or some other measure. This will nearly always work out much more expensive than all the other options, so they won't choose this one, but it shows that you're willing to take a risk and work with them	Partnership option	(e.g.) £2 per hour of staff time saved

The details will vary according to your industry, but this is one example of how to construct a bespoke quote without going through a time-consuming analysis every time.

When it is time for a face-to-face negotiation, the psychology has a lot in common with pricing approaches, but some of the subconscious messages that you usually convey through pricing can also be put across directly in the negotiation. After all, your pricing structure conveys your confidence in the quality and value of your product; it shows that you are willing to be reasonable and tailor the price to the budget of your client, as long as they accept the appropriate tradeoffs in features or benefits; it allows you to defer the client's pain to the future or shift it onto someone else; and it demonstrates that you can walk away from the negotiation because you have other clients who are willing to pay for your product or service. All of these factors apply in a negotiation, and your actions and demeanour should be consistent with them.

This means that you go in confidently with your price, making no apologies for it. If the customer asks for a discount, you only offer it to them in exchange for some reduction in the benefits of the service. The reduction in benefit may not be exactly proportional to the reduction in price – you need to judge how important saving money is to the client relative to the other benefits you offer. You should be creative with offering solutions that delay payment to the future or tie it to pain-free events like increasing the client's market share. If they push you too far you need to be willing to say no (though you can play safe by saying no on a small point, to gauge how much they are willing to bend, before taking the risk of walking away from the whole project).

You might even find some of the same techniques apply when you're negotiating a raise or a bonus from your employer.

There are whole books on negotiation, both with your customers and with your boss, so I won't attempt to provide a full treatment of the different techniques. But the basic psychological points are the same as for pricing: understand and take control of the expectations of the other party; give them a choice between several options on your terms, not theirs; and make the payment distant – emotionally or in time – but make the benefits close, visible and highly salient.

Chapter 11

The tea party

Inspired by a visit to the USA during the Congressional election campaigns, Maggie launched her range of luxury products in May with a new marketing campaign: the Chocolate Tea Party.

Having gradually built up a mailing list of several thousand loyal customers over nine months, the company announced a competition to select the top 100 influencers. They each received a visit from someone in the sales department and a gift of the new luxury tea range. This combined an exclusive high-cocoa chocolate with a range of Japanese and Chinese teas, served in a handmade pottery tea set.

The range was not designed to be enjoyed alone, however. The tea set came with eight small cups and saucers, and the quantities were made for sharing. This was the launch of the Chocolate Teapot Company's first social marketing experiment.

I took a trip to Liverpool to visit an early summer tea party hosted by influencer number 37, Joanne Spiers. Joanne was a charming lady of indeterminate age (let's be polite and call it 45) whose house by the river had a beautiful, secluded garden. She had set up a tray for tea and cakes before I arrived, and invited me to sample a little before the party proper got started.

We sat together on the grass, with a small table in front of us, and Jo opened a packet of luxury Cho-Chai. The tea was sealed in a thick parchment packet and the chocolate, disc-shaped, wrapped in a cacao tree leaf. She placed the leaves in a porcelain pot and poured some boiling water over them. A timer chimed after 90 seconds and she dropped the chocolate discs in.

Another minute and she poured the tea out into two small china cups. We could almost have been in Kyoto instead of Liverpool. I brought the tea to my lips, anticipating something special.

It had a lovely flavour, more delicate than the normal teapots and with a sweetness that was more subtle. Instead of the normal strong black tea, which needed a fair hit of chocolate to balance it out, these teas tasted more herbal, with only a hint of chocolate providing some warmth in the background. I savoured it for a few moments before taking a bite of sesame-infused rice cake.

With hindsight, I realised how strongly my experience of the flavour was affected by the power of the ritual and of all the extra attention I paid to the flavour as I tried it. The very fact that I knew this tea was expensive made me enjoy it more.

Jo's guests arrived soon after, and I watched their reactions to the tea as well as the interactions across the table throughout the evening. I've never been to an Avon or Ann Summers party but I imagine they might be a little like this, if more risqué – some gossip, some trying out different products and comparing them, and all the while a careful social comparison of who's buying what.

The social dynamic was fascinating. Everybody clearly felt they had to buy something. Jo told me she had invited only people who would be comfortable with spending a certain amount of money, but I wondered whether some might just make a token purchase. It seemed, though, that they all wanted at least one luxury tea set and a range of cakes to go with it. When someone reached the £100 mark the others all added enough extras to take them over £50.

The distinction instead turned out to be between those who were interested in hosting a party themselves and those who chose not to. Three of the guests also placed an order for stock and all the required items to host their own tea party – which they did not need to pay for until after they had hosted it. Jo was to receive some kind of commission on whatever her guests sold at their own parties.

I noticed an intriguing effect halfway through the party. A series of luxury porcelain teapots had been provided with the party pack. Each matched one of the cups from which the *guests were drinking. Jo passed the teapots around during the evening, and everyone had a chance to pick out the teapot that matched their cup and see how they looked together. The people who had physically touched each pot were more interested in buying them at the end of the party. Each guest, once she had looked at the pot and handled it, seemed to put a higher value on it than did those who had not touched it.*

In the end, people were sufficiently unwilling to give up the teapots they'd tried that Jo sold over £600 of products at the party. Two more parties were booked and one more was to be arranged. Rolled out across the country, this marketing channel looked like a good bet as a sales source in itself and also as a way to introduce newly launched products to the market.

Two powerful effects are at work together in this chapter, as well as a few more minor ones.

The first is the **peer effect**. In situations where we have little past experience or guidance as to the appropriate way to behave, there is a strong pull to follow the example of other people like us. Part of this is because we use their behaviour as a cue to tell us what a sensible strategy might be for ourselves. And part is because we don't want to look silly in front of our peers.

The peer effect can even override our own reasoning capacities. In one experiment, subjects were shown a series of lines on a screen and asked to say which was the longest.

Diagram 6

One of the lines was clearly longer than the others, and when shown the lines unprompted, 100% of subjects got it right. On a second test, new subjects were placed in a room with several other people, who unbeknownst to the subjects were actually part of the research team. The researchers all pointed to a line which was clearly shorter than the others, claiming – against the evidence of everyone's eyes – that it was actually longer. In about half of cases, the subjects went along with this and pointed to the wrong line too.

When there is no clear right answer – for instance, how much tea should I buy, how much should I spend, or how much should I contribute to sponsor my colleague's marathon run? – the effect is even stronger, especially when our decision is visible to our peers: we have an interest in behaving like them, to reduce the risk of embarrassing ourselves or them.

This can be seen clearly in social marketing contexts such as the chocolate tea party, or to some extent through social media such as Twitter and Facebook. It also works in retail environments: when a person sees other customers buying a product, they consider it to be a justification of both the price and quality of the product. Recommendation engines on websites work on this principle – 'other people who liked X also bought Y' – although it is not clear whether they use price as one of the criteria for their recommendations.

A related effect is **reciprocity** – where people who have been given some unconditional gift or assistance are likely to reciprocate by spending more money in return, or making a purchase they might not otherwise have made. In many party marketing contexts there is an expectation that the guests will buy a product as a gift for the host. The purchase of this gift may also help wary customers to get past their inertia: once the first purchase is made, others will follow.

The **subjective quality** effect was also seen in this chapter. The fact that the luxury tea set was priced higher than a standard tea led to a direct improvement in the experience of the customer.

This is a well-known effect with wine. Subjects tasting a wine which they believed cost £40 per bottle enjoyed it much more than the same wine which they were told cost £7. The reasons for this effect are not fully understood, but they may be related to the length of time and attention the drinker spends savouring the wine; it may be fulfilment of an expectation of high quality, if the drinker starts with the assumption that the wine will taste good (or bad) and then adjusts slightly upwards or downwards based on its actual taste. Drinkers may even take particular identifiable flavours – for instance a high tannin level – as a sign of high quality in a good wine, and simultaneously as a sign of low quality in a bad wine. The same principle applies to many other products.

The second main phenomenon demonstrated in this chapter – also related to inertia – is the **endowment effect**. Researchers have discovered that people put a higher value on things they already possess than equivalent objects that they don't own or have not touched.

If you give out small objects like mugs or chocolate bars to individuals and ask them to look at and hold the objects for a short time, their valuation of those objects will increase. People on average will assign a 20%–50% higher value to the object they have been given than to similar objects that they have not been 'endowed' with. Thus, if offered the chance to trade these objects with the others in the room, they will be less likely to swap if they have held onto the object for a while.

This endowment effect is stronger if the objects have been physically touched, but it works even without that. It is related to the phenomena of **loss aversion** and the **status quo** bias. All of these effects arise from the fact that people prefer things how they are, and want to hang onto what they've got rather than taking the risk of swapping them for something uncertain.

Whether you can use these effects in your business depends on the nature of how you sell. In a retail environment, if you have sales staff who spend time personally with the customer, they can physically place an object into the hands of the buyer before asking whether they want to purchase it. This will increase both the likelihood that the customer will buy, and the price they are likely to pay for it.

If you sell by mail order, you may find it worthwhile to offer customers your product on a sale-or-return basis. Of course you may lose some when a few people do not return the product and do not complete payment (although by taking card details you can now eliminate much of this risk), but the chance that a person will want to keep the product once they have had it in their possession is much greater than the chance that they will want to pay for it before they have seen it.

If you offer a service rather than a product, the endowment effect suggests that you should consider encapsulating the service in a physical, tangible version. Customers who can 'hold the service in their hand' are more likely to think it is legitimate to pay for it than those for whom it is completely intangible. You do not want customers to become too focused on the likely cost of the physical object itself, so ideally it should be symbolic of a larger experience rather than encapsulating the whole service fully in itself. A good example is that, alongside a physiotherapy service, you can offer exercise equipment which the customer can use to practise what you have done with them. Some objects can be very cheap to provide – a rubber strip or ball, for example – but can offer a lot of intrinsic value in complementing, and providing a reminder of, your service.

How to apply it

Social effects have the most powerful effect when you can bring together people who are loyal and regular purchasers of your product with those who are not yet committed to it, or not willing to spend so much.

Look at your customer segments and see which of your customers have the highest willingness to pay. Can you identify any social context where those people are likely to be in the company of others who do not fit that segment? If not, can you create this context yourself (as CTC did with the tea parties)? You may be able to set up seminars where existing or likely customers can meet with others who have not yet started to buy your product or service.

At these events, provide products at a range of different price points, but try to incentivise your high-spending customers to make a visible purchase from the expensive end of the range. You could do this by directly offering the host a commission on sales, or by simply asking them in person to do it. Customers who rate your product highly are often quite happy to help you out if you ask.

The subjective quality effect is most useful when you remind customers of the high price they have paid during the experience of consumption. Try providing cues in packaging or in the way a service is provided which reinforce the price message. This might involve investing in some services or features which are technically unnecessary – for instance a dentist might provide a private waiting room for their patients or a personal followup call after an appointment to ask whether the tooth still feels OK – but which are designed to remind the customer that they paid more than is standard and that they are being indulged accordingly.

The endowment effect is easier to apply with a product than with a service, but symbolic objects can be provided as part of a service offering too. Look at your value chart and determine which objects would most clearly encapsulate the values that are most important to your customers.

Consider whether you can find a mechanism to give customers the object before they make the decision to buy it. In a face-to-face sales environment this is usually straightforward. You can also let them select their preferred product and then offer them a slightly more valuable version – a higher-quality product or one with more capacity or features. The customer will often perceive that there is no downside in trying out the upgraded version of the product. Once they have tried it, they will experience a strong resistance to downgrading to the version they originally intended to buy.

Chapter summary

■ If people are unsure about a new product, or whether they should pay a certain price for it, social approval is a powerful way to reassure them.

■ You can promote this by bringing different customers into contact with each other – those who are less price sensitive and already willing to pay a higher price with those who have not yet been willing to try it.

■ Giving people a product to hold physically will increase their attachment to it and make them more likely to buy it.

Chapter 12

Bundling

One Sunday in June I realised that I'd grown to rather depend on my chocolate teapots. I felt like drinking one, but opened the cupboard to find there were none left. At 10pm it were too late to go out and buy one. But I realised that there were a couple of squares of white chocolate in the corner, and some teabags. It was time to carry out an experiment.

I boiled the kettle and picked out the tea which seemed most similar to the Assam variety that CTC uses. I poured the water into a cup and, while it was still boiling, dropped in both a teabag and a square of chocolate. I had to keep stirring for a while before the chocolate would dissolve, but eventually it worked. Cautiously I raised it to my lips to see how closely I had managed to replicate the chocolate teapot experience.

Pretty close, it turned out. The tea was more bitter than the CTC variety, and there wasn't quite enough chocolate, but it wasn't a bad approximation. It was a little more work and a little less elegant than the official version; and a lot cheaper.

I worked out what the ingredients had cost me. About 6p for the teabag and 5p for the chocolate – far less than the 60p it would have cost in a supermarket. Admittedly there was no teapot with it, but did I really need one?

I emailed Maggie to discuss. Her reply came back within a few minutes:

From: maggie@chocolateteapotco.com
Subject: Re: homemade teapot
Date: 19 June 22:35

Hey Leigh

Sure, the ingredients are cheaper on their own. Though
you can't get exactly the same varieties of tea and
chocolate as we source them direct from the growers. It's
all about bundling. You can take away a whole category of
price sensitivity by combining more than one product
into a bundle which is different from anything else on the
market. Have a look at your mobile phone contract.

Best
Maggie

Mobile phones are indeed one of the clearest examples of bundling. The companies know that their basic service is a commodity — a one-minute phone call on one network is not very different from a one-minute call on another. If they sold all their services by the minute, it would be very easy for customers to simply compare one price with the other and pick the cheapest. Each network would lose most of its business if it didn't cut its rates to compete — and soon enough, all the networks would be operating at breakeven point and making no profit. (If you've studied economics, you'll recognise this as **competitive equilibrium** — the point where all suppliers are fully competitive and none makes any profits. A major role of the marketing function in any company is to make sure this doesn't happen.)

Networks avoid this competitive pressure by bundling a range of services into one contract. Take the most basic offering you could imagine from a mobile company:

- 13p/minute for calls within the UK

Now compare it with a typical (actually, a fairly simple) contract from a real network:

- Handset (iPhone 4 16Gb) cost £89, or £129 for 32Gb

- 900 minutes of free calls to any network or land line in the UK

- Calls charged at 10p/minute thereafter

- Calls to non-geographical numbers charged at 25p/minute

- Unlimited free texts (subject to reasonable use limit of 3,000 per month)

- Additional texts charged at 12p each

- Picture messages at 35p each

- Texts to overseas at 24p each

- Receiving calls abroad costs 19p/minute (within the EU)

- Making calls abroad costs 38p/minute (within the EU)

- Variable price in other locations, from 20p to £2/minute

- 750Mb internet data allowance per month

- Additional data charged at £5/500Mb

- When travelling within Europe, 25Mb/day data allowance

- Outside Europe, £5/Mb for the first megabyte each day, £3/Mb thereafter

- Minimum contract length 24 months, eligible for handset upgrade after 18 months

- Contract costs £40/month (including VAT)

Is £40/month a good price for that deal?

If you can answer that, you're a step ahead of nearly everyone else in the country. And if you try looking for exactly the same package from another mobile provider so that you can compare them on price — well, you won't find it. There are so many permutations of services that, regardless of whether the networks were to collude or simply put bundles together randomly, the chance of finding exactly the same deal elsewhere is vanishingly small.

One reaction is to add up all the individual components and try to calculate the total value. But this is very difficult to do accurately. How much is a text message worth to you? The answer is probably different depending on whether you're on a night out forwarding a joke to a friend, setting up a date with a new partner, or stuck on a mountain trying to get rescued. And how many messages will you use this month? What's a phone call worth to you? How about the chance of having a better signal when you're travelling to meetings in another part of the country?

Because these things are impossible to work out accurately, you fall back on rules of thumb. Once we've made the decision that we really need a mobile phone, we use some basic approximations to figure out whether this particular phone is a good deal.

Does it have a reasonable number of free text messages included in the plan? Well, where do I fit in the range of text-message users? Personally, I see myself as a low to medium user: I can imagine that the 3,000 text messages in this package are designed for teenagers who use text as a basic communication protocol; but the alternative package with just 500 texts might not be quite enough — better safe than sorry. How often will I go abroad? A couple of times a year, but that might increase during the two years of the contract if I do more business in the USA and southern Europe. How much data will I use? I have no idea, but 750Mb seems to be the most they offer, so I guess that will probably cover me.

This process is called **satisficing**, a word coined by decision theorist Herbert Simon to combine the ideas of 'satisfying' and 'sufficing'; we satisfy ourselves that the product suffices to meet each of our needs. Once we have checked that the basic features of the product are likely to roughly meet those needs, we then check the price. Sometimes we use price as a way to estimate value because there are so few other accurate ways to quantify the benefits of a product. In a case like this, price may become a fairness check — 'Am I getting a reasonable deal?' rather than 'Is this the optimal package I could buy?' In any case, I can always ask myself: 'Will I get more than £40 of value out of this phone each month?' The answer is undoubtedly yes.

Most businesses do not want, or need, the bundling complexity of a mobile phone contract. But you should consider it as a way to change the conversation in your customer's head.

If you sell a product or service which is easily compared to that of your competitors, customers can play a game against you. You'd like them to think about whether your product is worth enough to them to justify the price. Usually your £3 product will create enough value to be worth substantially more than £3 to the customer; a ratio of 3:1 is typical, so that the customer gets £9 worth of benefit from your £3 product. If they think about it in this way, they should be happy to pay £3.

However, if there's another product very similar to yours, the customer will not focus on the total value of what you offer; instead, they will fixate on the price of the competitor's product. If the competitor is selling for £2.50, they'll expect you to charge £2.40 — the competitor will have to cut their price in turn, and in the end you will both be driven down to the lowest possible cost and make no profit. Most customers are not overtly aware of this game they play, but it is implicit in how they buy things.

How to apply it

The way to defeat this game is to make sure that your product can't be directly compared with that of a competitor. And bundling is one of the best ways to do this.

By adding extra features to your product, you will defeat the competitor who wants to undercut you: but, more importantly, you will defeat the subconscious tactics of your customers. Have a look at the benefit matrix you built in Chapter 1, and work out how you can fulfil those values by bundling additional, low-cost product features or extras.

A credit card company – whose values include convenience, deferral of cost, and whatever emotions are associated with their brand – could tempt their customers not to compare on interest rates alone by bundling:

- free air miles or similar usage-based benefits

- insurance for purchases made through the card

- discounts on holidays or other services from partner companies

- free roadside assistance if you hire a car with the card

and so on.

A fast food company might – and most do – bundle several complementary parts of a meal together into a single purchase. The classic example is the hamburger, chips and drink; usually these are priced at a discount of 50p–£1 to the price of the individual items. A key point here is that the prices of the individual items are nearly always visible to the consumer – there is a strong expectation of fast food merchants that they should offer each item as a standalone option as well as in a bundle. Thus, the bundling offer is quite transparent and this constrains the freedom of the retailer.

They must be careful to ensure that the price of the three-item bundle is less than the three individual items, but more than the price of any two of them. Otherwise people who want only two of the items will save money by buying the third. Although it doesn't cost the retailer much to serve a free drink to buyers of a hamburger and chips, it disrupts the psychological purchase rationale presented to the consumer.

An accountant – whose values include compliance, reduction of stress, tax savings, reduction of workload and security – could differentiate their product by including:

- free insurance against tax investigations by HM Revenue and Customs

- a free tax audit to find and report on the key areas where the customer can pay less

- free online accounting software to reduce the data entry burden and allow a faster turnaround of the annual accounts

- free company secretarial and registered office service.

Most of these services are offered by most accountants anyway. But they are usually tempted to split them out as individual options, each with its own price. This destroys the power of bundling. It enables customers to compare, line by line, each of the services with the price from competitors – and to drive down the price of each of them. Instead, the accountant should wrap all of these services up into a single fee – a fee which will be higher than the cost of each item added together.

Should you charge more or less for a bundle than the cost of individual items?

This is a common question asked by people designing product bundles. In the Chocolate Teapot example, the bundle price is much more than the competitive price of the individual components (11p). While in the mobile phone contract, the price is (probably, though it's hard to tell) cheaper than the price that would be calculated by adding up the individual components.

The short answer is: if you have high fixed costs and low variable costs (like the mobile phone networks) your bundle should be cheaper than the cost of the individual services, because it encourages people to buy and use more of the service. If most of your costs are variable (like the teapot company) you should use bundling as a way to increase the total margin you can achieve per sale – and thus charge more for the bundle than the individual products.

A bundle price higher than the sum of its parts will be more persuasive if the parts reinforce each other and jointly create a value which would not be present in either component on its own. For example, in the accountancy case, having all of your information handled by one company saves time and negotiation and reduces the number of potential mistakes. The chocolate teapots create a joint experience which (for those who enjoy it) is preferable to either the tea or the chocolate on its own.

Note the use of the word 'free' in the list of bundled services above. This will be the subject of the next chapter.

Chapter summary

- Bundling is a way of differentiating your product from competitors' products.

- Bundling also makes the cost of the product harder for customers to work out, giving you more control over the value that customers perceive in it.

- A bundle can give customers good value for money, especially if you have high fixed costs and want to increase total quantity of usage, or, in a service context, if most customers are likely to use some items in the bundle and not others.

In focus

Name your own price

It seems strange to let the customer choose the price for a product or service, when this is normally one of the supplier's main strategic choices. But in some scenarios it works.

There are three different versions of this approach.

The most spectacular, but probably the riskiest, is to provide a service or product to the customer and ask them afterwards to pay whatever value they put on it. A few restaurants occasionally use this method, and the band Radiohead had success with it for their album *In Rainbows* in 2007. Some theatres in London use this policy one night of the week. And in a sense, this is the model used by museums which ask for a donation of your choice, and service providers who expect you to leave a tip at your own discretion. The success of the approach depends on a strong culture of trust and goodwill existing between you and your customers, and runs the risk of exploitation if the product's marginal cost is high. And customers will usually seek some kind of anchor price to guide them on an appropriate amount to pay – so it may be useful to display a 'recommended price' or some examples of what other people have paid.

The second is to let the client make an offer, and then decide whether to sell your product to them or not. This model is used by the website Priceline, and in a way is reflected in the standard employment model, where a company advertises the salary it is willing to pay and waits for applicants to show up. It tends to drive suppliers into tough price competition with each other and may be a good idea for the customer but probably will not make a viable business for the supplier. Many hotels and airlines use Priceline to get rid of last-minute inventory which they would not otherwise sell.

The third is to let the client tell you their budget – most common in a business-to-business situation – and then tailor your service or product to fit it. In many public tenders the client will provide a guideline price. This may backfire, as it can encourage cheaper suppliers to raise their prices to use up the whole budget. But as a supplier it takes away much of the price risk in your negotiation. This approach by a client reduces the likelihood of suppliers competing on price — they will tend to cluster their prices close to the stated budget. As a supplier, you might sometimes do well by lowering your price to around 10% below the budget, as this is likely to be as low as anyone else will go. In general, submitting multiple price options is a good idea even in response to a formal tender — this gives the client options and a degree of control which they are unlikely to have with most of your competitors.

Except for the last of the three variations, this kind of approach is unlikely to form a stable business model for most suppliers. But for promotions, spare inventory or low-marginal-cost extras, it can be a useful part of your pricing mix.

Chapter 13

Free offers

In July I managed to collect 23 teapots and pay for none of them.

I did it as a bet with myself, but also to experience the range of promotional offers that CTC had been launching in the last few weeks. It felt like Maggie might be planning something. But she hadn't been available to meet me, so I thought it might be time to use my research skills and see what was going on myself.

It started three weeks ago . . .

I visited my usual Cosanostra Coffee for breakfast and bought my usual chocolate teapot – vanilla with white/milk chocolate blend was the variety I'd been fond of recently. With my receipt was a loyalty card. I'm sure you know the kind – they give you a stamp with each purchase and when you have collected 10, you get a free drink.

This one was different in one detail – instead of 10 spaces, it had 12. And instead of stamping just the first space, the cashier stamped the first three.

X					

X	X				
X					

I smiled at Maggie's ingenuity. Although the card still needs the same nine more purchases to get my free teapot, the three stamps seemed to create a "sunk cost" effect, which made me feel a lot closer to the goal.[1]

Although I have about 15 of those loyalty cards sitting around in my kitchen drawers, I rarely change my buying behaviour based on them, except when they're already nearly finished. But this month I found myself using that card again and again, and before the end of the third week, I had free teapot number one.

My second free pot was in the supermarket. I stopped in on the way to the office to pick up a teapot to drink when I got there. But when I looked at the shelf, there was a special offer there which I hadn't seen before: buy two, get one free. I decided I couldn't miss the chance for another teapot, so I picked up two more and took advantage of the offer. I ended up drinking two of them at the office that day, so the offer had persuaded me to consume more than I normally would have. And when I looked at the receipt, I realised that the price of the teapot had gone up from 89p to 99p. So keen was I to get the free offer, I hadn't even noticed the change in price.

Having got myself one free teapot and started on the path to another, I thought it would be a cute game to see how many more I could pick up within the month. By now it was 10 July, so I challenged myself to somehow get hold of a free teapot every day for the rest of the month. With two already in the bag, I needed 23 in total.

The next time I saw an offer was at a bookshop, of all places. I went along for an author signing – the new travel book about Tajikistan by one of my favourite authors – and the shop was offering hospitality, as well as an autograph, to buyers of the book. They'd discovered that one of the CTC teas was grown in the Tajik mountains, and, according to the store manager, CTC had been happy to do a good deal on 36 teapots. The shop was

---

1. An experiment by Joseph C. Nunes and Xavier Drèze showed that giving consumers a two-stamp head start on a loyalty card at a car wash – even though the advantage was illusory – increased the number of people completing the card by over 80%.

able to sell a fairly expensive, quality hardback book without discounting, and customers seemed pleased to get the free gift. There was a clear consensus among the other customers that online bookshops – even if you can save a few pounds – don't offer free tea with their orders.

Number four was not exactly a free teapot but free tea, as I got a large pot for the price of a medium. I asked for an orange-flavoured pot in a different chain café – I was travelling and not at my local Cosanostra – and they offered me a free upgrade to a large pot if I bought a cake with it. So I had a slice of lemon tart (quite good with an orange chocolate tea, if you ever have the chance to try it), got my large pot, and ended up staying in the café for two hours writing an article. I bought lunch there and they ended up making twice as much money out of me.

Number five was a voucher offer in a magazine. When filling it in I noticed the opt-out box but decided that since they were offering me a free teapot, the least I could do was let them send me some advertising. The principle of reciprocity is strong – you scratch my back, I'll scratch your free scratchcard – or something like that. I got my free teapot in the post two days later and that was me on the CTC mailing list.

Number six was when I discovered – from that mailing list – that CTC was now offering home delivery. Free delivery with any order of four or more teapots was tempting, but what was really interesting was the reverse offer. They had partnered with a same-day delivery service. And if you paid for the delivery service, the teapot was free. I decided to indulge – partly to rack up another free teapot towards my month's target, and partly just for the hell of it. Sure, it cost me £6.50 – but have you ever had nothing in the fridge and just wanted to have someone bring a freshly poured drink to your door? Well, I did. And it was worth it.

By this time I was wondering why this flurry of offers seemed to be surrounding me all at once. I managed eventually to get Maggie on the phone.

"It's all strategy," she insisted. "You'll see in the end."

"Give me a clue, at least. You can't be having to offer discount deals to shift your stock, surely?"

"No, no!" She seemed keen to reassure me. "Demand is higher than ever. This isn't a desperation move in any way. It's just about getting to a bigger market. People are wary of drinking something they don't recognise, and a free offer is one of the best ways to get more people to try something new. In four weeks we've got over half a million new people to try us out. If we manage to hang onto a tenth of those as semi-regular drinkers, it pays for itself six times over."

Teapot number seven was a limited-time promotion from a newly opened local sandwich shop: come in on opening day and get a free teapot. Again a useful tool for the shop – letting local office workers know they are there – and for CTC, who won some new tea drinkers and a loyal retail outlet. The goodwill that CTC won by offering a couple of hundred free teapots, which cost them perhaps £40 in manufacturing expense, was far more than they could have achieved by paying the shop. Free gifts are a good way to create a positive mutual obligation between you and another business, and they have much more symbolic value than plain cash.

Number eight was an extra that the CTC retail staff threw in when I visited the factory on a research trip. I went to the factory shop to buy a gift for my mother, and at the checkout the cashier added in an extra teapot – cinnamon and dark chocolate – as a gift. Once again the goodwill this created will be worth much more than the cost of the teapot, and it introduced me to a new flavour I probably wouldn't have tried on my own. I might buy it again.

Numbers nine to 22 came as part of an impressive promotional offer. Once I was on the mailing list, they emailed me a special offer: an automated Teasmade-style alarm clock and kettle. Imagine! Being woken up each morning with a freshly made teapot. And, best of all, it came with two weeks of free teapot refills, which meant that the purchase paid for itself in teapots alone. So I ordered one, set it up and now I am woken each morning by the delicious smell of tea, chocolate and – importantly – caffeine. That in turn helped create an even stronger tea-drinking habit, and no doubt will lead me to buy more teapots in the next year than I would otherwise have done. I even signed up to a subscription plan to receive five teapot refills each week in the post.

I won't count the free biscuit I got with my ginger teapot in Manybucks last week, though it did lead me to buy the teapot without looking at the price. Nice biscuit.

And number 23 was part of a bundle of free stuff that I got in a hamper sold by the local deli. I did have to buy the physical hamper, for about £19, but in it there was a chocolate teapot, some cake, biscuits, honey and a bunch of other stuff – I have no idea what the cost would have been to buy it all, but it was very tasty.

So I won my bet. And while I did get a whole month's worth of free teapots, I don't think any of the companies who gave them to me have lost out.

Why do free offers work so well?

Many purchase decisions involve more than one component. Order a book online and pay a delivery fee; buy a main course and then pay for a side dish and drink; sign up for an accounting service and decide whether also to buy their annual company secretary service or separate tax advice.

When this happens, the consumer could think about the purchase in one of two ways. They could add the components together and consider: is the total purchase worth the money I'm being asked to pay?

Or they could think separately about every item and make a separate evaluation of each. On the face of it, this is illogical – because they can't buy the delivery charge separately from the book it comes with – but it turns out that is what a lot of people do.

The danger in this is that if the consumer thinks the delivery charge is too much – even if the overall deal is a good one, because the book itself is cheap – they may decide not to buy.

By asking them to make two decisions, you create twice the opportunity for them to say no to your offer.

Including add-on items for free – or, more accurately, including them in the price of the basic product – makes it easier for your consumer to say yes, by taking away a decision. The word 'free' signals to a consumer that they don't need to think about this item at all. It's free – no downside – therefore you can focus just on whether to buy the main item at the price charged for it.

Two well-known case studies – there are many more – show the power of free offers.

One, carried out in the laboratory by Dan Ariely and colleagues, offered people the choice between a cheap chocolate candy for 1c and a luxury truffle for 26c. Most people chose the 26c truffle. When another set of subjects were offered the choice between the cheap candy for free, and the truffle for 25c, they overwhelmingly switched their preference to the free one.

Another was an experiment accidentally conducted by Amazon. In most countries Amazon offers free delivery for orders over a certain value, or, during some temporary promotions, on all orders. In France, the delivery charge was not free but was set to one franc (this was in the late 1990s, before the euro). This is a tiny amount of money compared to the price of most books, so one might expect it to have almost no effect. Nobody would consciously dispute that a franc is a fair price for delivery. And yet, this small change resulted in far fewer sales. When free delivery was offered in France too, sales increased significantly.

How to apply it

This is one area where you can, and often should, move away from the value comparison chart that you developed in Chapter 1. The key values of your customers are those which they will pay for. Free offers are most effective in the dimensions which customers do not value so highly.

135

For example, if you sell a car and your key values are comfort and reliability, your existing customers may not place a high value on excitement. Therefore offering a free holiday might attract new customers without diminishing the value placed on your main product features.

'Free' subconsciously communicates to your customer, 'get the upside without having to think about the downside', so it increases the appeal of a product with no penalty and without making the buying decision any more complex.

The drawback of free offers is that, for many customers, the free addition will not increase the perceived value of your product. Thus it may not increase the price point you can achieve with these customers, but you may end up giving away the free item anyway if it is offered alongside your main product or service.

You should therefore find free items to offer which have a low cost per sale to you. This might mean giving away something that has little direct cost, such as an ebook or an entry to a competition. It might mean partnering with a company that wants to promote its product to your customers. Or it might mean requiring customers to register or send in a voucher to get the free offer, in which case it will be taken up by only the subset of customers who most care about it.

Thus, seek out complementary products which are low cost and do not directly satisfy the key value dimensions of your main offering. If you do happen to find a product which does strengthen one of those dimensions, you may well be able to offer it as a chargeable upsell item (see the next chapter for details) instead of a free offer.

Alternatively, you could make your product or service the free offer in someone else's sale. If you find a company which is selling a non-competitive product into a similar marketplace to yours, and you want to get hold of some of their customers, try offering them a deal. They will be increasing the appeal of their own product, so they may be willing to pay you a contribution towards the cost of your product. You will gain exposure to a new market and a friendly new partner for future joint promotions.

Chapter summary

- 'Free' is almost a magic word. It transforms the customer's decision context from the default position of having to balance tradeoffs – is this feature worth giving up that one? – to one where there is no decision to make, because they get something for nothing.

- If a free product is bundled or linked with a priced product, it makes people better disposed towards the priced product.

- Free products can increase the urgency of a purchase, as consumers don't want to miss out on the chance to get something for free.

Chapter 14

Upselling

I went to see Maggie in August – the supermarket deal and café distribution were settled, sales continued to rise steadily – and asked her what was next.

"You tell me," she replied. "What do you like to eat with your chocolate tea?"

I thought about it. "Quite often a croissant; sometimes a biscuit. Usually I don't eat anything, I suppose."

"There's your answer, then. We want to capture some of that market – or create more of it."

"Are you manufacturing your own biscuits now?" I asked.

"I wouldn't get into that business," she replied. "Too risky to invest in setting up all the kitchens and so on. Fortunately there are people who already took those risks. Have a look."

She showed me several products, branded with "Chocolate Teapot Company", which were distinctly not chocolate teapots. One was a chocolate-covered ginger biscuit, one a Danish pastry, and the others different variations on the theme.

"Isn't this just line extension?" I asked. "The marketing gurus say line extension is a dangerous thing – it dilutes the brand."

"Agreed – but we don't expect anyone to buy these on the strength of the brand. These are our new premium revenue

source – to let us capture a higher share of wallet when a teapot is being drunk."

I looked up at the wall of the factory café and there were some new items on the menu.

- Chocolate teapot: small £2.59

- Chocolate teapot: large £3.09

- Add a G-Tea ginger biscuit: + 79p

- Add a D-Tea Danish pastry: + £1.89

Now that I saw it, the pastry did sound like a tempting way to soak up some of the tea.

"How many of these are you projecting to sell?" I asked.

"We've done some testing already. The original goal was to do more price differentiation – giving price-insensitive people an extra route to spend more money. But we've realised this also helps us capture part of the audience who would have bought food anyway, but from someone else. Looks like we'll increase sales by about 15% in the outlets that are willing to stock the extras."

"So if you wanted to create more price differentials, why not just increase the price of the top product?"

"It can be tricky to do that. Although we always run a high-priced option alongside our core items, if we move the top price up too high it can affect the overall perception of value for money. If people see a £6 teapot on the menu, it hurts us in two ways. First, it shifts up the average price point for teapots, so if people are choosing between teapots and coffee, or even deciding whether to enter the café at all, they are less likely to do it. Second, it changes people's assumptions about the low-end products. They may assume that if the top price is £6, the £2.59 option can't be any good. So you can only use differentiation and anchoring up to a point."

I was surprised by this. "Didn't someone do some research about jury trials where they found the anchor always had a positive effect, no matter how high it is?"[2]

"Yes, but that's a slightly different situation," said Maggie. "In that case, the jury had to make an award – they had no alternatives open to them. We are in a competitive market and people can buy a different product altogether if they don't like us. If they think of us as being an expensive product, they may unconsciously avoid us before even noticing that we have some affordable options as well. But if we use optional products to differentiate, the customer doesn't perceive those prices as part of our product – even though they may end up spending nearly £5 instead of £3."

I was starting to understand the complexity of pricing perception. Low prices attract customers to even consider your product, or your shop, as a buying option. Once they have made that decision, you want to influence them to pay as much as possible, without going so high that you completely put them off buying. And then you want them to remember your product as being good value, so that they come back again to buy more. All this while managing the margins of other companies in the chain – retailers if you're a manufacturer, or manufacturers if you're a retailer, or complementary service providers if you offer a service.

There's more on how to profitably handle this complexity in Chapter 17, "Managing the pricing environment". For now, though, Maggie had a specific problem.

"We want to get our café channel to sell our biscuits and cakes with our teas, rather than the other products they stock. So

2. This research by Chapman and Bornstein was carried out in a mock courtroom. The experimenters described a lawsuit to several juries made up of volunteers, giving identical details about the scenario, the victim and the guilt of the defendant, but with one key difference. In some cases, the prosecuting lawyer asked for a compensation award of $100; in others $20,000; and in some cases $5m or $1bn. In every case, the higher the request, the higher the award – even when the amount requested was a patently ridiculous sum like $1bn. To be sure, the juries did not award anywhere near the amount actually requested, but a $1bn request still got a higher result ($490,000) than a $5m request ($440,000).

James is trying a few experiments. We'd like to know what you think."

Maggie introduced me to James, an earnest young man with curly hair, wire-rimmed glasses and a somehow incongruous white lab coat.

"OK, look at this now," he started. "Maggie's explained to you about the biscuits, right? Well here are our different biscuit plans; let's see what you like best."

I was back in the product test room where I'd first encountered the chocolate teapots several months before. On several tables were a range of teapots with different products lined up beside them.

First, a regular milk chocolate teapot, price label £1.99. Beside it, a chocolate biscuit priced at £1.20 – reduced to just 75p if bought with the teapot.

Next, a bitter chocolate teapot, price label £2.29. With this one, a caramel biscuit at 65p.

Third, a large white chocolate teapot, priced at £3.35. Beside it, a scone and butter for £1.60.

James explained to me the reasoning for each.

"There are two different ways to do an upsell. One is to extract more money from people who want more of the same thing from the product. The other is to offer something complementary to broaden the appeal of the product.

"The chocolate biscuit is the first kind. It's designed for customers who want even more sweetness and will pay more for it. They can get a certain amount of sugar in their tea for £1.99, and an extra hit for 75p more. And they save money too! The other two options are about activating different attributes. People who prefer the bitter teapot might still want a little sweet flavouring to complement it. The scones are for people who are drinking tea to satisfy their thirst, but are feeling hungry too."

"And the pricing?" I asked. "Why is the caramel biscuit cheaper than the chocolate one?"

"I can't give you a scientific answer to that, I'm afraid. We are just trying out some different price points for different attributes. Different customers have different preferences, and people who like the taste of bitter tea seem to care less about sugar than people who buy sweet tea. The scone combination seems to work well when the total price comes in under £5 – so we've kept it just under that level."

James added in a low voice, "Don't tell everyone, but the guy who owns Cosanostra was round here last week and he loved the scone. Sir Charles something or other."

I assumed this was Sir Charles Leverkraft, chief executive of Leverkraft & Gamble. How interesting.

When I visited a café the following week I noticed the first offer, the chocolate biscuit, was available at the counter. I didn't pick one up, but halfway through my teapot I felt like it might be nice to have a bit more sweetness. Why hadn't I bought it with the teapot and got the discount? Sighing, I went up to buy it anyway – and was pleasantly surprised when the café discounted it to 75p regardless. It felt like a gift. Another nice touch to increase my loyalty to the brand.

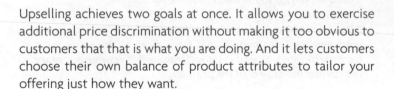

Upselling achieves two goals at once. It allows you to exercise additional price discrimination without making it too obvious to customers that that is what you are doing. And it lets customers choose their own balance of product attributes to tailor your offering just how they want.

This technique applies perhaps even more to services than to physical products. The experience of a service is more complex, and typically there are more attributes for variation. You also have much more customer contact while providing a service, and many more chances to complete the upsell. Customers who do not realise they want the extra service right away might change their minds later.

There is an important difference in the decision-making process between buying two items at once and buying them separately.

If buying the teapot and biscuit together, people are likely to add both prices together and subconsciously compare the total to the size of their usual purchase. If the teapot is bought alone, the price of the biscuit then seems much smaller – relative both to the teapot and to the innate thresholds within our minds. These thresholds vary from one person to another, but a purchase of less than £1 or less than 50p is evaluated by many people as a trivial decision, barely worth thinking about. Sometimes, therefore, you can more easily sell a product at £1.99 and another at 75p than both together at £2.74.

The thresholds will be different for services, and for business purchases. For example, a hairdresser whose main service is a wash and cut at £40 could offer an upsell based on the experience of the cutter – a senior stylist at £50 or a salon director at £70. Or they could add extra services or products: a head massage for £15 or a bottle of salon-quality conditioner or mousse for £12. Once the main purchase decision has been made, and is treated as a **sunk cost**, the additional purchases will be perceived as relatively minor, inexpensive ways to enhance the experience in comparison to the original purchase amount.

A software company that has sold a £30,000 project to its client will probably be able to sell several additional features at £2,000 to £5,000; again, in comparison to the project size, the additional features are cheap. And there are similarly likely to be decision-making thresholds – perhaps below £1,000 or £500 – where the normal processes that can slow down or veto a purchase are suspended. Sometimes these are formally laid down in the organisation's policy, and sometimes the limits are more informal, based on the instincts of the decision-makers in the company.

How to apply it

Examine the benefits and value tables from Chapters 1 and 3. You should by now have a clear idea of which product versions are strong on each value attribute.

In contrast to the free offers in the previous chapter, you should choose upsell opportunities that *do* match the key value dimensions of your product or service.

Look at the value chart and choose one of your products that satisfies some of the value dimensions but not others. Then choose one of the values that is not provided by that product.

When someone has bought the product or is in the process of buying it, you can then offer them extra items that satisfy the missing values. As these are optional, you can set a high margin on them without increasing the perceived price point of the core product. Even if only a small proportion of customers choose to take up the optional item, you are likely to increase margins significantly.

Take one of your key products and list in the table below the values that it satisfies. For each value where it is strong, look at what new item you could add to intensify this value. For example, a chocolate biscuit to intensify the 'sweetness' value of a teapot, or a head massage to intensify the 'pampering' value of a haircut.

Then look at values where the product is weak, and look at what you could offer that might improve the product on those dimensions. Typically the upsell on weak dimensions will achieve a higher price than that on strong dimensions, but this is not always the case – you will need to test against real customers to find out how much they are willing to pay.

Product	Price	Values	Upsell item	Add-on price
Teapot	£1.99	Sweetness (strong)	Chocolate biscuit	75p
		Hunger (weak)	Scone	£1.60

Use the following blank chart for your own analysis, or visit www.psyprice.com to download more blank templates.

Product	Price	Values	Upsell item	Add-on price

Chapter summary

■ Once someone has invested in your product, the opportunity to enhance it with (relatively) low-cost add-ons is very attractive.

■ Upselling can give you a way to intensify the product on any of the value dimensions that you have defined: for example, for customers who like the sweetness of tea, offer a chocolate biscuit that is even sweeter.

■ Upselling makes your price discrimination more effective, giving wealthier people a way to spend more money with you.

In focus

Occasional versus frequent purchases

A major question in the behavioural economics research literature is: do these psychological effects last a long time, or do they disappear quickly as people visit the same shops or interact with the market frequently? Maybe Starbucks can get you to spend £5 on a latte the first time you visit, but once you realise they're available for £2.50 elsewhere, competition will start to work in the way we'd expect and prices will be driven down.

There's certainly some truth in this. The better you know a market, the standard commodities for sale and the prices they sell for, the more you are likely to behave like a 'rational' consumer. If you are buying something unfamiliar, you have less information and you are more likely to be guided by the unconscious cues of positioning and relative price.

But do these 'learning effects', as the literature calls them, eliminate all the effects of pricing psychology? Not at all.

The approach in this book is mainly designed for those who are selling a product into a market of regular purchasers. Some parts of it, in fact, only work when you can both create a first impression and then reinforce it, training your customers to know what to expect from you through consistent positioning and brand communication over a period of time. The chapters on 'positioning' (Chapter 1) and 'memory' (Chapter 6) are all about how to first create these impressions by leveraging customers' knowledge of existing categories, and then sustain them by being consistent each time they encounter you.

However, some techniques do work particularly well for one-off or unusual purchases. Imagine a customer is in a new environment, say a music festival or West End theatre, and they want to buy something. Perhaps the product is also unfamiliar — a souvenir brochure and DVD — or perhaps it's something they regularly buy but in a different context — a glass of wine. In both cases they will have little idea of the appropriate price, and use of techniques such as anchoring and decoys will be very powerful. It is relatively easy to get someone to pay a high price when they encounter something for the first time. I recently paid over $10 for a cup of diet Coke in a theatre on Broadway, and I'm supposed to be trained in this.

Customers' defences are down in these situations. They return to a more natural mode of behaviour: the simple consideration of whether a product provides enough enjoyment to be worth paying the price asked. It takes away the strategic consideration that consumers always subconsciously apply: 'Is this a good deal? Could I do better somewhere else?' This is partly because there often *is* nowhere else, and partly because they have a lack of information about the situation they are in.

This doesn't mean that consumers will forget about it afterwards. I certainly don't feel that theatre was generous to me with their $10 Coke, and I will keep telling people about it. But it probably won't stop me going to the theatre; and even if it did, that particular theatre probably would not mind — they have their $9.80 profit from me already. If you have the courage to take the money and accept the perception of being expensive, go for it.

If, on the other hand, you want customers to believe they've got a good deal, and come back to buy from you again, you need to be more careful. If they can compare your product directly with that of a cheaper competitor, even after the fact, you may lose their future business. This is one reason why the 'positioning' chapter is so important: make sure that you differentiate your product or service from low-cost competitors, and anchor its value to that of a more expensive category.

Don't let your product be seen as a commodity. Sell the teapot, the chocolate biscuit and the tea all together so that the combination is unique. Turn your legal services into a membership subscription with a unique combination of options, distinct from what any other law firm provides. Or sell books, but sell them with an interactive review section on your website, and the option of a face-to-face meeting with the author, and the possibility that readers will be mentioned in the sequel. This way, you get to control the perceived value of your product, and all the techniques in this book will keep working, no matter how many times the customer has bought from you.

Chapter 15

Absorption and value pricing

I didn't see Maggie for a couple of months that autumn. She was travelling a lot and when she got back she seemed preoccupied with a lot of financial meetings. But I did see a lot of teapots.

She seemed to have struck distribution deals with at least one train company and one airline; I saw teapots on their menus on more than one occasion. The prices were higher than the price points at retail, I assumed because of the need to pay a margin to the transport company.

On one of my visits to the factory while Maggie was busy, Sandra from the marketing department stopped by her waiting room. She spotted me and invited me to have a walk with her and look at some of their new strategies. It would be nice to have a new face in my article, so I gladly took the chance to speak with her.

As we walked towards the marketing office, I asked about the deal with the airline.

"I can't tell you the exact percentages, but they don't take a much higher margin than any other retailer. It's our decision to raise the price in that market."

"Because they're captive and can't go elsewhere?"

"Not really. We wouldn't want to risk the brand by making people feel exploited. Here's the reason why we do it."

We arrived at her office and she found a chart in a filing cabinet.

What you spend on holiday:

- Flight: £400

- Hotel: £600

- Taxis: £150

- Meals: £525

- Chocolate teapots: £7.18

"Easy to see the point now, right?" she asked.

I nodded. "In fact, the teapot looks almost comically cheap now. Don't people want to spoil themselves a bit more when they're on holiday?"

Sandra smiled. "Yes they do. And as it happens, we have developed the perfect product for them."

With a clear sense of pride, she opened a box – covered in metallic foil – and pulled out a teapot in a colour I hadn't seen before: orange.

"Are you driving, by the way?"

I shook my head. "On the train this time."

"Good. Fill it up then."

As I poured hot water into the teapot I could smell the familiar aroma of tea leaves and lightly melting white chocolate. But this time there was something else: an orange aroma, and a sense of something sharper, more pungent.

A minute passed; I poured from the pot to a fresh cup and sipped. A flood of warmth abruptly filled my mouth and stung my throat as I swallowed, slightly taken aback. "Has this got alcohol in it?"

Sandra smiled. "Yes, this is our Tea Cocktail. We nearly called it a Cocktea, but that seemed kind of risqué – especially in the plural. It sells for £9 in-flight or £8 on the train. We find that consumers who have paid over £100 for their flight don't see a £9 extra purchase as expensive. We try to communicate the price as part of the whole package. And if you travel in first class on the train, we have an agreement with the train company to include the price in the ticket instead – which makes people even less price-sensitive."

I could see the potential. Tea Cocktails in a hotel minibar would work well – next to a £200/night hotel, £9 more for drinks is insignificant. Maybe in restaurants too.

Sandra nodded. "That's our next rollout – we think the restaurant market will be huge for us. Incidentally, there's an anchoring effect as well – when we sell regular teapots alongside the Tea Cocktails, we can get £4 for them – much more than the standard price."

How to apply it

To apply this in your own business, you will probably need to find another company to partner with. Choose one whose product or service sells for much more than yours – for instance, if you're a removals company, try working with an estate agent; or if you sell a software package for £50, talk to a shop selling computer hardware at £1,000.

The other company needs to attract the customer: there's no realistic way for you to translate your customers' desire to buy software into a requirement to spend 20 times more on hardware, so the relationship is going to be asymmetric. Once they have an interested customer, who wants to spend £1,000 on a computer or £350,000 on a house, your purchase will appear relatively small and they will be much less price-sensitive.

You still need to distinguish your product from the alternatives with other attributes – quality, taste or functionality – but the customer will be more willing to pay a higher price for these attributes than if the product is sold on its own.

The more important sales job, in fact, may not be on the customers themselves but on the partner. You need to show them how offering your product to their customers will be in their interest.

Often they will expect a margin on sales, and in the case of the airline and the Tea Cocktails, they certainly would. However, this is not always true: some professional service firms, for example, prefer not (or are not allowed) to accept sales commissions.

In all cases you should consider how your product will enhance the customer's experience of the partner's product. The removals company should show the estate agent how working with them will make the moving process easier and less stressful. The software company should make sure that they choose a computer hardware partner whose target market fits their product. Your goal is to help the partner turn their product from a commodity into a unique product or experience.

You should work hard to present your product in turn as a distinctive, non-commodity offering. This will have the same effect on the partner as on the consumer: when seen against the price of their more expensive product, the quality attributes will become relatively important and your price less so. This leaves you in a stronger negotiating position to maintain your margin: the partner may otherwise want to push you down on price, either to improve their own profit margin or to use you as a sales promotion to attract more customers.

In some cases you can apply **absorption pricing** yourself without partnering. If you sell a variety of different products at diverse price points, you can use this approach to reduce price sensitivity on the lower-valued products. This has the same effect as upselling (see Chapter 14).

Alternatively, you can position your product in a channel where it is likely to be bought alongside a more expensive item. When your product is an accessory for another item – for instance car tyres – this is natural and easy. Otherwise, you have to be creative. A book about marketing might be sold next door to an expensive business seminar. Or a hair straightener could be offered to buyers of prom dresses.

Case study

Software company

XSQ, a small software firm specialising in selling to car leasing companies, was unsure whether its licensing model of a one-off fee per user was the correct approach.

Smaller clients had been pushing back on paying the full licence fee, and XSQ had a suspicion that some of them were sharing logins in order to get the benefit of the software without paying the proper price. On the other hand, some larger clients were paying the licence fee without question, and XSQ felt there might be room to charge them more. The question: how to design a model to capture more from the bigger clients without losing all the small ones?

XSQ examined the high-level values of its clients:

■ increased residual value on post-lease vehicles

■ winning more customers

■ leasing more cars

■ achieving higher margin on each car.

They realised that none of these values were closely related to the number of employees using the XSQ software package.

This created a distance between the pricing policy and the way they communicated value to the client.

Using a new project with an existing client as a pilot, they tried linking the price to the amount of financial value generated through the software. They created a measure of financial margin per vehicle and average residual value, generated some statistics for the previous year and created some spreadsheets to measure the same statistics for the coming year. XSQ asked for 30%, but, after negotiation, the client was willing to pay only a 12% share of the additional value generated.

Over the next year the money started to come in, but XSQ had to sit down with its client several times to renegotiate details of the deal. It turned out there was a high demand that year for smaller cars which would naturally have a smaller residual value anyway, so XSQ wanted to adjust the formula to take that into account. And market interest rates rose, meaning that the margin on finance automatically increased – inevitably, the client wanted to rewrite the deal to reflect that.

XSQ would have tried to include these factors in the price the next time it worked with a client, but some other unpredictable variable would have interfered with the next deal. But what really made this model impractical was the fact that the ultimate payback could not be calculated until well into the future. Some cars are not returned from a lease deal for three years or more, and the residual value cannot be finally calculated until then. So XSQ had to wait several years for full payment for its software. This was survivable in a pilot, but would have badly hurt cash flow if applied across all of its clients.

But then the marketing director came up with the idea of combining a **value proxy** with **absorption pricing**. Instead of trying to calculate the exact value generated by the software, XSQ worked out an approximate figure, which worked out at between £30 and £110 for each car leased, depending on the value of the car and the length of the lease agreement. Then they looked at the business process of the client to find out where they were spending money anyway.

Two types of transaction dominate the financial model of a leasing company: the £7,000–£20,000 they spend each time they buy a car, and the £500–£1,000 they receive in commission from a finance company when they sign a lease agreement. These therefore seemed to be the right places to charge the fee. XSQ worked out a simple licence fee per car model, charging an average of 0.5% of the value of the car, part payable when the lease agreement was signed and part in a quarterly licence as service payments were received from the end customer. This meant that XSQ's client was never out of pocket, and in some cases was even able to pass the software licence fee on to its own customers – using the principle of **other people's money**.

This model enabled small leasing companies to manage their cash flow and pay only for the value they were getting, while larger ones ended up paying a higher share of the development costs of the software. XSQ found it was able to charge an average of 40% more through this method than with its previous model.

Common applications of this technique:

- selling drinks alongside meals in a restaurant

- selling food and drinks with a long-distance travel service

- accessories sold with a car or computer.

Case study

Marketing consultant

CH is a consultant working on marketing projects for clients. Primarily she is a copywriter, helping her clients choose the right words to communicate their message, but she also gives some advice on brand strategy and the visual design of marketing materials.

CH, like most consultants, uses the traditional pricing structure of a fixed rate per day (with some negotiation depending on the client).

Typically consultants using this model can earn between £350 and £1,500 a day. (The upper end is hard to reach for individual consultants, but achievable for many consulting firms.) CH has been earning at the lower end of the range, between about £350 and £500 per day, and sells about 50% of her time.

This model reflects the cost of providing the service for the consultant, but does not recognise the value gained by the client. Using an advert designed by CH, a client might generate £2m in new sales, but it may have taken her only two days to write and therefore she earns only £800.

There are three reasons why the day-rate model is appealing in this sector.

First, it reduces the risk to the supplier. Consultants who price according to goals achieved or value generated take a certain amount of risk – will the goal actually happen? If it doesn't, they may have worked for nothing. A day rate means that the consultant knows how much they will get for each day worked, regardless of results.

Second, because most consulting services are to some degree bespoke, it can be hard to create a general model that represents client value. This is especially true for highly generalised services such as management consulting. One week you might work on improving customer service standards for telephone staff; the next week, on developing processes to create new relationships in a reseller channel; the next, you are advising on business planning to raise investment funds. The value generated by each of these jobs is very different, and this makes it both hard to measure (developing value measures might take as long as doing the actual consulting) and hard to standardise on a common definition of value.

Third, because clients are often not concerned directly with value, but instead with whether they are getting 'a good deal'. Where there is no other measure of how good, or fair, a deal is, clients find it easy to understand day rates. There is an established range of prices for consultancy day rates (as suggested above) and any rate outside this range can look unfair. It is easy for a client to extrapolate from a £4,000/day consulting rate to £800,000/year of income, and to ask whether their supplier really should be earning that much. Conversely, a £100/day rate equates to £20,000/year and the client may start to worry that the supplier undervalues themselves, and this can be a warning signal. So day rates give the client a simple way to evaluate how fair, or sensible, the supplier's business model is, and in turn offers the client the power to negotiate a lower price. It also lets clients believe they are comparing competing consultants on a like-for-like basis, even though this is objectively almost impossible to do.

Despite these pressures, a value-based charging method is a much more powerful mechanism for a consultant to use. If your client makes £1m out of the process improvements that you help them implement, you should aim to find a way to charge £100,000–£200,000 for this service. Of course, this has the downside that if you make them only £10,000 you may be paid only £1,500 in return. But if you don't have the confidence in your skills to be sure of achieving your client's goals, should you be taking the job?

Not only is this (arguably) a fairer way to apportion the benefits of the work, but it has some direct beneficial outcomes:

■ It incentivises you to take the jobs that will generate the most value, and turn down those which will not – which is better for economic outcomes, and for your clients, and ultimately better for you.

■ When you are carrying out a project, it guides you to spend your time on the activities that are most valuable, and to eliminate or minimise time-wasting tasks and meetings.

■ As a result, this model is both better for you – because you'll make more money – and better for your clients – because you'll do a better job for them.

It isn't always easy to implement a value pricing model. The two big difficulties are defining measurements, and persuading your client to accept it.

Client persuasion can be tough. Clients often think that if you want to change from an established pricing model it's because you want to charge them more money. You can point out some of the arguments above, but they may say that you should already be doing the best job possible for them, and that is what they are paying for.

The best response to this is to reposition your service. Easier with new clients than old ones, this means describing what you do, not as a consulting service for hire but as a kind of product offering. You want them to think of you not as a replacement or competitor to an existing service, but as a new way to solve their existing problem. The solution to CH's pricing dilemma relies on this **reframing** decision.

If you want to pitch this to new clients, you may need to offer them a day-rate option as well, so they do not feel you are forcing them down a route they don't want to take. It may be most effective to offer this new model to them on an especially risky project – perhaps one that they're uncertain whether to pursue. The results-based or output-based method might make the difference between going ahead with the project or not. And once the precedent is established, it will be easier next time.

It is often hard to objectively **measure the value** you create as a consultant, simply because so many other things are changing at the same time. If you help to redesign the marketing message for your client, and afterwards their sales go up by 10%, is that because of your work? Or is it because they increased their advertising budget, or hired a new and talented salesperson? You usually can't ask the client to cease all other changes in the business in order to measure the effects of your work, and unless they are a big company with many customers and a strong commitment to measuring their marketing efforts, they won't be able to split their sales messages and accurately compare performance between the two groups.

So you need to define proxy value measurements. By this I mean variables that are objectively measurable and which are a close representation of the value you create.

The solution to CH's pricing problem was the following.

- Analyse the values of her clients: winning new customers; improving their brand image, selling more stuff to existing clients; improving conversion rates.

- Convert those into measurable outcomes: successful adverts.

- Charge £2,000 for an initial strategic consultation, which can be fully offset against future adverts if they decide to use CH for future work (the offsets are limited to 25% of the price of the advert so that she doesn't end up doing a lot of free work).

- Charge £750 per advert she writes that the client chooses to implement. At draft stage, the client is given the choice whether to go ahead; if they do, she creates the full advert and the client pays when they publish it.

- Charge £100 for each time the client re-runs the advert. This gives her a stake in its success. What's more, it gives her an interest in revisiting the client to help test and improve the advert in the future. This is a good way to sell the client on the benefits of a value-based approach.

Chapter summary

- Attaching or comparing the price of your product to something much larger can make it easy for customers to buy without thinking.

- If you can show that your service enhances the experience, or profitability, of something much bigger, this comparison will look more convincing.

- You may be able to earn extra revenue by linking your reward to a percentage of the value of a bigger item, especially if you are selling to businesses.

Chapter 16

Other people's money

I was in a car, being driven along the M4 by Rajiv O'Brien, who described himself as CTC's head of enterprise sales. It seemed hard to picture just what an enterprise sale of a chocolate teapot might look like, but Maggie had suggested I go with him on a client visit.

A couple of briefcases rode with us in the back seat, and Rajiv asked me to carry one of them into the client's office, which we reached just before Bristol. I sat beside him as he started his presentation to the client.

"How productive are your staff over the course of a day?" he asked.

The client, Hannah Michaels, the HR director of an insurance company, didn't know.

Rajiv pulled out some charts showing average productivity of office staff throughout the course of a day. There was a peak from about 9.30am to 11am, and another short one from 3pm to 3.30pm. At other times, the chart reached no more than half the peak heights.

"This graph shows how much work people produce at different times of day. It corresponds to the blood sugar levels of the employee, which influence their ability to concentrate."

I won't repeat the whole presentation. The point turned out to be that chocolate teapots – and more generally, a carefully managed schedule of tea, coffee and food throughout the *day – was good for health and good for productivity. Rajiv ended up pitching a service combining consultancy, employee advice and provision of daily teapots.*

He asked me to open the briefcase. Inside were five different kinds of teapot, designed for different times of day, with or without sugar. Alongside them sat a manual and an iPad – on which he demonstrated a software program that tracks the employees' time and alerts when they should be putting another teapot on. It all looked very slick.

"So we can demonstrate that an employee on this programme can be 15% more productive – which, on your revenue figures, means an extra £75 per day for every employee. Plus, you improve your corporate responsibility rating, and get more loyalty from your staff. For this we charge only £9 per day per employee. What do you think?"

Hannah clearly found it difficult to disagree with the figures, though she claimed not to be able to make a decision without approval from the board. Rajiv suggested a pilot programme.

"How much can you approve without going to the board? Would they make you wait for a board meeting to spend £1,000 a month?"

"I suppose not. What would we get for that?"

"We could run a pilot for three months with a team of 10 staff. I'd be giving you a discount but I'm willing to do that if you agree to evaluate it after each month to see whether it should roll out to the rest of the staff."

Hannah thought for a minute and agreed to give it a try.

On the way back, Rajiv explained some of what just happened.

"First and most important, she is spending other people's money. We wouldn't easily get anyone to put £1,000 of their own money into something untried, but when the money belongs to the company, the pain of shelling it out from your own wallet is not there. In fact, people can make more rational decisions – based on costs and benefits – with their employer's money than with their own.

"Second, I used monthly payments, anchoring, absorption, per-employee pricing and a trial period – all to reduce her sensitivity to the size of the payment.

"Third, I gave her a clear rationale for the purchase. Maybe she doesn't believe, in her gut, in the productivity figures. But now she has a clear rationale if her decision is questioned by anyone else in the company. In fact, she can argue that the potential productivity gains across the whole company are so high, and the cost of the trial so low, that she wouldn't be doing her duty if she didn't try it."

Three months later I checked in with Rajiv. It turned out that the pilot had been a success – the 10 selected people were 10% more productive [note: I suspect the Hawthorne Effect,[3] but that's a different story] and the insurance company had placed an order for all 400 of its staff, which worked out to over £600,000 per year. "Not bad for a few cups of tea," as Rajiv pointed out.

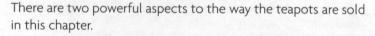

There are two powerful aspects to the way the teapots are sold in this chapter.

The first is that a product has been converted into a service – with some intangible expertise bundled in, and made tangible through the physical teapots and the software tool. Tangibility is an important aspect of pricing; it is easier for people to make a decision to buy something if they can feel it in their hand – it gives them a clearer idea of what they are buying and can help to remove a source of doubt.

3. The Hawthorne Effect occurs when workers in a company know that a new scheme is being tested on them, and that they are being measured – and in response, their productivity increases regardless of whether the scheme works. It was first noticed in a factory where the managers wanted to test whether brighter lighting would improve productivity. They turned the lights up – and sure enough, production went up. Four weeks later the experiment was over and they turned the lights down again – and production went up again! This is one of the reasons it's important to design your experiments correctly, with randomisation and "double-blind" techniques so that you don't inadvertently measure an effect which isn't really happening.

Tangible objects also give rise to the **endowment effect**, a psychological phenomenon whereby people value something more highly once they have held it in their hands (explained in more detail in Chapter 11). This is related to **loss aversion**, which means that the pain of losing something you already have is greater than the pleasure of gaining an object of equivalent value. Both of these can be used to good effect in making people put a higher value on what you sell.

The second effect comes from **other people's money**. In this example, Hannah Michaels is spending her company's money, not her own. You can see the same effect when toyshops sell to children, who are not price-sensitive because the money being spent usually belongs to their parents or grandparents. Of course, price is still an issue – the object being bought must be perceived as worth more than the money spent – but the fact that someone else's money is being used removes a whole series of psychological barriers to purchase.

A lot of what prevents us from buying things are cognitive factors: fear of making a mistake; the potential regret of buying something that wasn't as good as we expected; worry about looking silly; or the indecisiveness that comes from not knowing the experience we will get from a purchase. It is much easier for a business purchaser to get around these issues and move the decision on to concrete grounds.

There are other challenges in selling to businesses – they are more likely to look at competitors, less likely to be influenced by deferred payments, and their decisions may be less influenced by the intangible value that we create through anchoring and decoys. But these effects still work, even if not quite as strongly as on personal purchases.

How to apply it

Your business may already be committed to selling only to consumers or only to businesses. In this case, the decision has mostly been made for you. But you can still find ways to move the conversation in the right direction.

If you sell to consumers, there are three main mechanisms you can use.

1. Create a purchase that can be made by a third party. For example, jewellery is often bought for its wearer by their partner and not by the wearer themselves. De Beers famously promoted diamonds as the standard for engagement rings in Europe and the USA throughout the course of the twentieth century, and eventually managed to create a (somewhat chauvinistic) price expectation, that men buying an engagement ring should spend one month's salary on it. Recently I have heard someone trying to suggest that two months is the new standard. Shameless, but I have to admire their chutzpah.

2. Show how the purchase can be absorbed into, or netted off against, a third-party spend. For instance, if you sell new furniture, this can be incorporated into the process of buying a house, and financed by slightly increasing the amount borrowed on the mortgage. The consumer feels like they're spending the bank's money instead of their own, so it becomes easier to make the purchase.

3. Find a business justification for the purchase, and show buyers that they can claim it as a business expense.

4. Develop a way to sell it to businesses directly. To do this, you should go back to the benefit and value tables from Chapters 1 and 3 and look at additional value that could be gained by businesses. You can be quite creative, as CTC was with its enterprise productivity service; or it may be as simple as offering your product as an incentive that companies can give as a gift to their customers or employees. In any case, the values involved in this decision will be different from those at play in a personal purchase.

If you already sell to businesses, you may want to look at how to make your product especially attractive to people who are not owners of the company. How can the HR director, or the chief financial officer, or the head of sales, improve their career prospects by buying from you? What are the metrics and statistics that might be important to them (productivity, lower tax, meeting their annual budget or sales targets)? What ammunition can you give that will enable them to confidently buy from you and defend their purchase to the board or the shareholders?

Chapter summary

- If a buyer is making a decision to spend money on behalf of their company (or some other third party) it takes away a lot of the emotional barriers to spending.

- There are still emotions present, however, particularly relating to the buyer's reputation, or their responsibility to be careful with their stewardship of resources.

- Once these barriers are overcome, the decision can become much more like the rational marginal-benefit decision of classical economics; it often becomes easier to upsell new features when their benefits can be demonstrated clearly.

In focus
Should you publish your prices?

This question is irrelevant for some businesses: in the retail world, and for most consumer products, your prices are on display and this is fully expected.

For others, this is a crucial question. In business-to-business sales especially, it's a major dilemma. Should you publish your prices on your website, so that your competitors can see them, as well as your customers, or should you wait until a customer asks and then give them a personalised quote?

There are different levels of transparency, too. Some businesses will send potential clients a price list if they call and ask, but do not want to include it on their website. A restaurant might include prices on its menu but will lay out the document in order to play down the price so that diners are less likely to use price as a factor in their decision.

The arguments **for** publishing are:

- it sends a signal of honesty to your clients and helps them trust you more

- it is seen by many people as a fairer approach, since they fear you may otherwise set the price according to how much you think they can pay

- it simultaneously qualifies out customers who are not willing to pay your price and attracts customers who are annoyed at your competitors' lack of transparency.

The main arguments **against** are:

- it makes it easy for competitors to undercut you

- you really *do* want to set the price according to how much you think the client can pay.

The right answer will depend on the market you are in and the competitive context. Sometimes companies collectively hide their prices until one competitor moves first and publishes, forcing the others to do likewise. If so, it's likely to be the lowest-cost company that starts off the process, as they have the strongest interest in encouraging buyers to compare on price.

Sometimes you can strike a balance by publishing, or emphasising, a low-cost option with the intention of upselling once the customer has started to engage with you. If you consider this option, be aware of the ethical and potential legal issues over 'drip pricing'. In the UK (in fact throughout Europe) there are rules against misleading pricing. See Chapter 19 for more information.

Occasionally you might do the reverse, publishing a high price with the intention of creating an anchor point, then negotiating down from it. However, this risks putting off customers who see only the high price and are not aware that they can negotiate.

On balance, if your salespeople or negotiators are well trained you can lose a lot of profit margin by publishing your prices. My inclination is that the best overall strategy is to publish a limited subset of prices if you need to do so to attract customers, but plan on negotiation and customised quoting to improve your margins.

Chapter 17

Managing the pricing environment

When I arrived at the factory for one of my last planned visits, at the height of an early English summer, the reception was empty. I could hear conversations behind various doors, and after waiting a polite length of time (six minutes) I knocked and poked my head into the open-plan marketing office. Everyone seemed to be in a panic. Whoever was not making a frantic phone call was in a very serious-looking conversation at one of the tables or around one of the many kettles.

I eventually attracted the attention of Sandra, whom I'd met a few months previously.

"We've just found out why our supermarket sales went up so much last month. Cosanostra Coffee have reduced their order by 80% this month. It turned out they managed to place an order via our supermarket sales team – and it's cheaper for them to buy the supermarket packs and open them up to sell in-store than to order directly from us."

"Ouch. Doesn't that create a load of work for their staff in unpacking all the teapots?"

"You'd think so, but apparently it's worth it. We sell in supermarkets at about £2 for four, so our wholesale price is 25p each. We've been selling to the café chains at about 70p a unit, so it's quite a big difference."

I listened in on some of the calls. Account managers were trying to find out whether one of the supermarkets had placed the order on behalf of the café chain, while salespeople were nervously chatting to other cafés, trying to figure out whether they'd had the same idea without tipping them off. The product design team was already working on how to differentiate the supermarket and café products more clearly.

Maggie saw me walking past the office and beckoned me in. She was on a call.

"OK, Valerie, very clever. I have to give you that. You beat us on this one. But we can't let it go on." She paused. "Well, if we have to we're going to change the supermarket packaging. We'll start by stamping 'Home Use Only' on the teapot. And when we can reconfigure the machines, we'll change the shape of the pots around." A longer pause. "Look, I don't blame you for doing this, but we can't sustain the channel at this price. I'll discount you the next two months' supply at the supermarket price, but after that we need to go back to normal . . . OK, drop me an email. Chat to you soon."

She hung up and smiled.

"I guess we walked into that one. All that trouble to differentiate our products between different consumer segments and we forgot to protect against the retail channels pirating from each other. Valerie Salmon has been waiting to get her own back on me and I guess she figured out how to do it."

"What will you do about it?"

"Well, as you heard, we'll start with embossing the supermarket teapots with 'Home Use Only'. A nationwide brand like Cosanostra won't be keen to have visible evidence on the product of how mean they are, so that will probably work for now. But longer term we will need to redesign the product a little more. We need to offer more concrete value to the in-store chain to maintain the price differential. We'll probably redesign the teapots so that the in-store versions feel like higher quality and the supermarket ones are more disposable. In fact, we've been thinking of a recycling programme already – maybe the cafés will end up with glass teapots which we will take back and reuse, and we will keep the supermarkets on plastic ones. Unfortunately our costs will probably end up higher rather than lower if we recycle, but it will be good for the brand."

"Has this kind of thing happened before?" I asked.

"Not exactly. But managing multiple channels is a challenge. It is part of the difficulty in designing the overall customer experience of our pricing, and for that we have to understand their decision-making processes. We have a flowchart for that – let me find it for you."

Out of a filing cabinet she took a bundle of papers, which unfolded into a large poster. It displayed a flowchart showing how consumers first experience the Chocolate Teapot brand, their perception of value and how it changes over time.

Diagram 7

Initial discovery	Advert	PR story	Supermarket pack	Café pack
Value anchor	Our control	Journalist choice	Yoghurt/energy drinks/premium snacks	Fresh coffee/tea
Comparisons	Focus on relaxation – compared with mug of tea, luxury environment	Positioned primarily against café products, depending on journalist	Other take-home snacks	Premium coffee products
Options	Prices not shown – range of options including multiple flavours and sales promotions	Up to journalist – encouraged to focus on lower- and medium-cost options	Single pack £1.39 Four-pack £4.49 Premium flavours 30% higher	Small: £2.29 Medium: £2.79 Large: £3.49 Premium flavours 20% higher
Triggers for re-purchase	Repeat advertising		Data capture	Loyalty cards
Reinforcement possibility			Regular supermarket visits	Regular café visits

"The important thing is to keep the value proposition consistent. We can't control exactly how the customer experiences our brand over time, so we can't risk creating any serious gaps in their perception. If the price or product attributes are very different across the different purchase channels, we will eventually lose out in one or more channels. In this case we were relying too much on the cafés themselves to create the distinction between our supermarket product and the café product. That gave the café the ability to capture too much of the price premium – we didn't retain enough control over the experience of our product.

"Another example of this complexity is the two-stage process that a customer goes through in order to buy our product. First they have to decide to buy it, and then they have to decide which product to buy. We need them to remember the product as an affordable treat, but then when they buy it, we'd like them to spend more on a larger or premium-flavoured teapot."

"And how can you do that?"

"There's no perfect way. People aren't daft – they will remember roughly how much they spent on our product the last time they bought it. But there are a few tricks. For instance, they will tend to classify products into approximate value ranges – for instance £2 to £3. Within that range, it is harder to remember whether you spent £2.19 or £2.65. If people buy a variety of different things on different days, the details will fade. This is one reason why the old £2.99 trick works – by charging £2.99 instead of £3, the consumer shifts us into a lower-value range without us losing too much money.

"Splitting the purchase into a teapot and biscuit is another way: even though they might spend £4.50 overall, the primary price of £2.79 is associated with the teapot. People subconsciously assume that when they walk into the shop they will just buy the teapot and not the pastry; but when confronted with the choice, they don't have that much self-discipline."

The scientific background to this chapter combines a few disciplines: the study of memory, cognitive dissonance, pattern recognition and game theory.

The formation of memories is complex but there are some principles which apply broadly. Repetition improves memory, so the more often people see your price communication, so the better they will remember it. More time spent looking at the information improves memory, so the longer they are in the environment, the better they will remember.

Pattern recognition is also a very intricate subject. The simplest message here is to be consistent. In each channel, present an image that reinforces the values that motivate people buying in that channel. Most buyers have little or no time to give much thought to what they buy from you; their first impressions will be powerful, and any further communication which contradicts those first impressions runs the risk of making the customer forget about you, stop recognising you, or stop considering you in their buying decisions.

The phenomenon of **cognitive dissonance** occurs when the customer is presented with two pieces of evidence which are apparently contradictory, for example if they remember you as a premium-quality supplier and they are suddenly presented with a scenario in which your product is the cheapest option. Cognitive dissonance creates negative feelings and makes people more uncertain – even fearful – and less likely to buy.

In most situations, you want to keep doing the same thing again and again, to reinforce the customer's perception of your product and increase the chance that they will remember you confidently when they make a buying decision. In some scenarios, brands can afford not to do this – for instance, the apparently deliberate price-blurring strategy of Coke and Pepsi, which we discussed in Chapter 6 – but these brands make up for it with immense pre-existing brand familiarity and very strong design and brand communication outside the pricing sphere.

Game theory is a way to understand the best possible strategy for each party in a competitive situation or negotiation where they are trying to get the better of each other. A full discussion of game theory is outside the scope of this book, but there are some recommendations in the bibliography. The key point is that it applies most strongly to parties who have the time to act 'rationally', by considering your interests and theirs, working out the strategy their opponent is likely to follow and responding accordingly. So game theory is of little use in understanding how a consumer buys a sandwich or a teapot, but it could be powerful in predicting the strategy of a major retail chain that is distributing your products. You can work out their main options, predict which will be most profitable for them, and set your pricing strategy and product range accordingly. If you can foresee – as in the CTC example – that somebody might have an interest in taking actions that you do not want them to take, you can adjust your own strategy to forestall this.

How to apply it

The principle here is to think a few levels deeper than your customer. In most cases, the customer pays much less attention to the purchase than you do. After all, they are only buying your product occasionally and have other things on their minds, while you sell it all the time, to many customers, and it is your job to think about how to do that better.

Think through the whole life cycle of how your customer experiences you. What is their first impression? What conclusions will they draw the first time they hear about your product? Will they compare it to something else? What are their instant conclusions likely to be? (And they should be instant, because chances are they will quickly forget about you.)

Then, the next time they see your brand, or your product, or are prompted to think about your category, will the message be consistent with the first time they saw it? Customers are driven on an instinctive level; they mostly don't have time to think logically through the process of buying your product. You have to plant the seed subconsciously that your product is the right solution to whatever problem or desire they have, and reinforce that until they can't forget it.

Much of that is done with branding and product communication rather than pricing. But the price is a very important clue to how they think about your product. And so you need to manage the price so that it is consistently communicated across all your different channels and in the different ways you communicate to clients.

Price arbitrage

Sometimes a price structure that is consistent for the consumer – in the Chocolate Teapot case, the difference between supermarket pricing and café pricing – opens you up to being 'arbitraged' between different channels. This can happen in two ways.

Professional buyers may spot a difference between channels and realise that they can take advantage of it. When someone is regularly buying your product, the effects of psychology are reduced and they pay more attention to the opportunities for profit.

Similarly, if you regularly have short-term sales, consumers may start to notice this and wait for the sale before purchasing. This is obvious in some industries such as clothing, where everyone knows that sales are coming after Christmas and in the summer, and many people wait until then to buy something which they might have been perfectly willing to pay the full price for.

If you sell a business-to-business service such as consulting or accountancy, once you have offered your client a discount, they know you are willing to work for the cut rate and it will be hard to persuade them to pay the full price next time.

So you need to defend your prices against each of these forms of attack. The most powerful way to do this is to create a product distinction each time you want to offer a discount. The Chocolate Teapot Company changed its product design for the supermarket channel, using plastic teapots while the café channel gets glass, clearly distinguishing the experience in a way that is psychologically consistent with the different experience of each outlet.

Some clothes retailers deliberately restrict availability of the most popular stock, to let customers know that by waiting for the sale they risk missing out on the garment they really want. And successful consultancies only offer discounts with a clear rationale: for instance, using more junior staff, or delaying the client's project to a later delivery date by fitting the work into hours that are not being used by clients paying full price.

Customers, even when behaving irrationally, still like to believe that the world is logical (this is sometimes known as the 'just-world phenomenon'). So give them a reason for a price difference and they'll be more likely to behave in the way you want them to.

You may recall the argument in Chapter 12 on bundling that fast food shops should ensure that their meal prices are consistent with the pricing of individual items. This is based on the same just-world rationale — it is counterproductive to confront consumers with an illogical pricing structure. This simply draws their attention to price in a way that you don't want. Paradoxically, for all the focus that you as a supplier should give to pricing, you don't want the customer to think about it at all.

Chapter summary

- Although it is usually more profitable to maintain different pricing points for different customer segments, this can allow third parties to *arbitrage*, buying at the cheaper price and selling at the more expensive price.

- Depending on the situation, you may not be able to directly prevent this, so you may need to make the product distinctions more visible, so that the third party is embarrassed into buying through the correct channels.

- Having control over the pricing environment includes shaping the customer's first impressions so that you influence the perceived value of your product.

Chapter 18
The psychology of giving

I received an email from CTC in December asking me to name my favourite charity. This question always puts me in a dilemma. Is it better to look at where the money will make the most impact, perhaps in cost per life saved; or at where it will provide the seed for a sustainable future, which suggests a microfinance charity; or at whether I can see the impact directly, perhaps a charity that a friend works for, or one based in my own neighbourhood?

All of these considerations have their parallels in the questions that come up when we buy a product: are we focused on the short or the long term, on getting the most for our money or on brand familiarity?

After some thought I submitted my suggestion: a microfinance charity covering sub-Saharan Africa. January came around and I noticed that a charity appeal started to appear on the supermarket boxes of chocolate teapots. For every teapot, 5p was to be donated to a charity. And inside every box was a code allowing me to go online and cast my vote among a list of nominated causes, with the donations to go to the most popular.

Every time I bought a teapot that month I was sure to visit the CTC website and vote. My nominated charity had found its way on there, though it wasn't the most popular – so I emailed all my friends to suggest they cast a vote too. Surely we could get enough votes together to knock that donkey sanctuary off the top position?

I talked to Maggie about the campaign. What had inspired it?

"You mean you don't believe that we're doing this out of pure generosity of spirit? Well, I suppose you're right. It's good for sales too. People are much more likely to respond to an offer of 5p to charity than if we simply took 5p off the price. Even though they could donate that 5p to whatever charity they wanted, it feels as though it has more impact when it comes off the profits of a faceless corporation."

"And the voting?"

"The voting is important because it gives people a sense of control. If you imagine donating 5p directly to charity, it would feel trivial – it is such a small amount, it's almost not worth giving anything at all. The feeling of influence from a vote on the destination of a £50,000 donation is much greater. Although the objective difference you can make is just as small, the vote allows you to believe that you are part of something bigger."

"Kind of cynical."

"Well, the objective effect might be tiny, but it does create a genuine feeling of loyalty between the consumer and the charity. It's a little like voting in a general election. The chance that your vote makes any direct difference is tiny. But the act of voting gives you a chance to affiliate yourself to a philosophy of life, and the knowledge that you participated in the democratic process is one of the things that help us all feel that society is working for us. This works the same way. You have signalled your support for the charity you care about, and there's a good chance that it encourages people to go out and support it in other ways too."

"Doesn't it run the risk that people feel they've done their bit, and they don't give any more?"

"That could happen. But you might have noticed that we tried to counter that by prompting people to make an extra donation after they have voted. We even match some of the additional donations ourselves."

"And how's it working out commercially?"

"Sales from that channel are up about 15%. Definitely worth it for us as well as for the charities."

Throughout the rest of the month I watched the voting totals move. My selected charity stayed near the top of the rankings, but those donkeys provided tough competition. I promoted the vote on Twitter, on Facebook, through my blog and with repeated emails to my increasingly annoyed friends; it seemed to make a difference, though presumably the donkey fans were doing the same. I can only imagine the sales of teapots to voters went through the roof – I bought 30 or 40 of them myself during the month.

As the 31st approached, the vote counts grew steadily. At midnight on the 29th, my sub-Saharan microfinance fund was on 44,200 and the donkeys on 44,350. By the 30th, it was 46,750 versus 46,795. And at 10pm on the 31st, 48,841 for Africa, 48,855 for donkeys.

I refreshed the website every few minutes to see the latest count. The tension sat somewhere in between the end of the football transfer window and presidential election night in November 2000. Was there any time left to influence the result? Had any of my friends bought teapots and not yet opened them? Was my local supermarket still open?

At 11.30 I decided to go out and buy their stock of teapots. After all, I was going to drink them the next month regardless. I might as well have a last chance to influence the vote.

There were 16 pots left on the shelf and I took them all. Four were premium Ecuadorian chocolate and cost more than I usually pay, but why not spoil myself for a good cause?

Back at the computer with 12 minutes to go, I ripped open each of the packets, pulled out the voting code and entered it into the website. The vote counts gradually crept up in both columns . . . 49,010 for microfinance, 49,015 for the donkeys – and I had only three teapots still to open.

Then a glance at my Twitter account told me I wasn't the only one doing this. "Microfinance", "teapots" and "donkeys" were all showing up in the "trending topics" list – apparently the vote had caught the attention of the social media crowd. My messages, along with dozens of others, were being retweeted again and again as the clock ran down.

I opened my last teapot, voted and refreshed the screen as 11.59 became midnight. The votes ticked over: 49,460 for microfinance . . . and 49,458 for the donkeys.

The next morning Maggie put out a press release thanking voters for their commitment (and, by implication, the thousands of extra sales that CTC must have made in the last week of January). They gave an extra gift of £10,000 to the donkey sanctuary as a consolation prize – which I suspect was planned all along – and the microfinance fund got £74,000. Each charity had also raised more than £30,000 in additional donations from voters.

When Maggie shared the sales figures with me later in February, along with customer registration details from the website, it appeared that the campaign had attracted around 30,000 new customers as well as the extra sales from existing consumers. As I learned later that spring, this must have been very helpful in some negotiations that were already under way at this time. The Epilogue reveals how those turned out in the end.

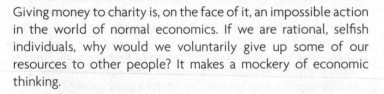

Giving money to charity is, on the face of it, an impossible action in the world of normal economics. If we are rational, selfish individuals, why would we voluntarily give up some of our resources to other people? It makes a mockery of economic thinking.

Of course, we often do give money away. In the UK, charities have an income of £26bn a year, of which 20% is from donations – about £100 for each individual in the country. And this is ignoring the much bigger 'gifts' we make within our own households – after all, do children do anything to earn the free rent and meals their parents give them every day?

Understanding why we give money to charity is crucial for the charities themselves, but it also sheds useful light on the buying process for companies of all kinds.

The most common explanation of charitable giving is known as the 'warm glow' effect. Giving money to charity makes people feel good. This rather broad motivation can in turn be broken down into the following.

■ People want to feel their lives have some positive purpose (a desire for meaning).

■ They want to feel connected with others (a social benefit).

■ They want to feel a sense of balance for selfish or negative actions (cancellation of guilt, or 'indulgences').

■ Some people feel that profitable companies ought to share their money, and charity is a way to redistribute it (political motivation).

■ Some want their generosity to be recognised by others (social status).

■ Those who have been giving to charity habitually may feel an impetus to continue doing so (habit and routine).

■ For some people, charities are about influencing other people's lifestyles in a way that they think is improving, perhaps by helping the beneficiaries become 'more like me' or supporting people who are already 'like me' (identity).

■ There are many other influences that can cause people to donate – religion, duty, guilt and more.

An important aspect of these motivations is that they are hard to measure. It is difficult to say whether £10 worth of guilt is much different from £5 worth; or will your friends be twice as impressed by a donation of £200 than £100?

The difficulty of putting a clear value on these benefits means that they are especially susceptible to influence by the techniques described in previous chapters. If you are designing a fundraising form for a charity, you can strongly affect what people give by changing the way you ask for their money.

Anchoring is especially powerful. If you first ask for £50, then suggest £20, donors are more likely to give than if you start out at £20.

Hyperbolic discounting works well – it is easier to sign up to give money later than to pay it now. This is one of the reasons why a regular monthly gift works well: £10 per month is easier than £50 today.

Free offers and bundling are effective too. If you want to sign people up for a monthly donation, try giving them a few different benefits in return. A newsletter, free entry to an exhibition, a badge or pen – whatever the offering might be (as long as it does not cost you much) it will expand the perceived value of the transaction and increase the likely donation level.

Social norms also make a difference. If you can show your donor that other people are giving a certain amount, it will create a strong pressure on them to match it. Given the lack of firm rationale for any specific donation, the existing behaviour of one's peers is perceived as good evidence for the appropriate action.

How to apply it

If you run a charity, you can follow the broader process described since the beginning of the book just as a profit-making business would do. Analyse the values of your donors, look at the positioning of your charity, the segmentation of your givers, the anchors that you create and the structure of deferred payments and bundles.

If you run a conventional business, you can still use the psychological effects of charity – as CTC did in this chapter – to boost your business and help a good cause at the same time.

Look at how you can make your customers feel good about buying from you by simultaneously giving to charity. The size of gift per purchase does not make a lot of difference – 5p in the case of CTC was little more than a token amount – because the emotional values which the consumer satisfies through a donation are hard to quantify.

You can also increase engagement with your product by a link with a charity. Most people care more about charitable causes than about your brand (which is not to say they care more about charity than about their own interests). An involvement with charity, such as the voting process used by CTC, might capture their attention better than some of your other marketing activities.

Look at your benefit matrix from Chapter 1 and the customer segmentation from Chapter 4, and think of what those values tell you about the different kinds of customer. What values are they likely to share that are relevant to charities? For some people, charity is about sharing their values with others; for some, the activities of a charity directly fulfil the donor's goals in life. If you sell financial services, you might find that a charity oriented towards microfinance will fit with your customers' attitudes of self-reliance and investment. If you make food, a charity whose goal is hunger relief might be a better match.

If you'd like to see how other companies are using this approach, look up Masala Masala. They manufacture fresh curry sauces, and from the proceeds of every pot the company buys a meal for an underprivileged person in India. Project 7, an American company, provides a broad range of products including water, mints and coffee. For each product, some of the money goes towards a charitable cause, for instance feeding hungry people in communities in the USA. Not only is the charitable benefit in each of these cases relevant to the product category (by buying food, you help feed someone else), but each company has chosen beneficiaries in a country which they feel will resonate with the values of their customer base.

Then examine your price points and see how a charitable contribution can either increase purchases or increase the amount people spend, without hurting your margins. You may well want the charity you support to achieve a certain level of income from the promotion, and this might affect the amount you choose to give. In any case, consider that the impact of a given charitable donation is likely to be greater than the impact of a price change by the same amount.

Tactically, charitable contributions can also be useful to smooth the way to a price change (a 10p rise in your price can be made more acceptable by a 5p donation to charity in the initial period of the new price point). They can also provide an advantage over competitive products or services which are otherwise similar to yours.

Some companies, instead of donating a fixed amount per purchase, set up a foundation and donate part of their profits or revenues to charity via that route. This can work, but makes the donation a less salient part of the purchase process. When the customer feels that their own choice of product has a very direct, tangible benefit to the charity, it is more likely to affect their buying decision.

Finally, charitable schemes often have a novelty effect, which may wear off after a time. Therefore you will probably want to run your scheme for a fixed duration. This can help to provide an extra last-minute sales boost at the end of the lifetime of the scheme, though there may be a small drop immediately afterwards as a few sales are merely brought forward into the promotional period.

Chapter summary

- Charitable gifts are often highly symbolic, meaning that the amount of money given or spent has little relation to the emotional value that the donor gains from it.

- The amount given is therefore less influenced by rational factors, such as value for money, than by expectations and social pressure.

- All the same psychological techniques that apply to regular pricing can be used, often with even stronger effect, for charitable giving.

In focus

How many pricing models are there?

This list isn't exhaustive, but if you want some inspiration for a new pricing approach, take a look at some of these and imagine how you can apply one — even if it seems unsuitable for your product or service. Some of these models can be combined (for example piecework prices with inflationary increases). Many of the techniques described in earlier chapters can be used in conjunction with these: anchoring, for example, can work with nearly all of them.

1. Flat, fixed product prices.

2. Bespoke quotes for each customer.

3. Monthly membership or subscriptions.

4. Percentage of value generated.

5. Percentage of some other number: asset value, size of transaction...

6. All-inclusive bundle pricing.

7. Cost plus a percentage markup.

8. Hourly rates for time spent (plus expenses or materials).

9. English auctions (with rising bids, as in an auction house).

10. Dutch auctions (with prices that fall until someone buys, as in the Amsterdam flower market).

11. Second-price auctions (eBay-style).

12. Industry standard pricing (e.g. equity rates for actors).

13. Piecework prices (e.g. a per-word rate for journalists or translators).

14. Annual contract with inflationary increases.

15. Component-based menu pricing (e.g. the Dell website).

16. Base price plus optional add-ons (e.g. most airlines).

17. Name your own price.

18. Demand-based dynamic pricing.

19. Advance commitment discounts.

20. Free to one group, supported by another (e.g. advertising-funded media).

21. Freemium (a free version alongside a higher-quality paid version).

22. Interest charges.

23. Penalty fees (e.g. bank overdrafts, parking enforcement).

24. Blade-and-razor model.

25. Income-based charges (e.g. some trade unions charge their members a percentage of salary).

26. Marginal cost pricing.

27. Discounting for market share land-grab.

28. Declining price as adoption grows (common for technology products).

29. Random fluctuations in price.

30. Temporary promotional sales.

31. Seasonal pricing (e.g. for holiday accommodation).

32. Quantity pricing (three croissants for the price of two, or £300 for a five-person licence).

33. All you can eat.

34. Competitive price matching.

35. Equity participation.

36. Retainers.

Chapter 19

The ethics and law of pricing

Maggie used to get letters every so often – not from customers, interestingly, but typically from people who had read about her in the business pages – challenging the ethics of the pricing tactics she used. Unusually, Maggie was fairly open about her pricing strategies. Most companies keep all pricing discussions behind closed doors, either from fear of competition or because they are worried that customers will not buy if they think their profits are too high. Maggie had given an interview to the FT explaining some of the approaches she used:

> We are interested in providing our customers with a whole cognitive experience. It's more than just a cup of tea; we want to encourage them to step aside from life for a few minutes, relax, enjoy the flavour and warmth of a drink, and pay attention to something inside themselves instead of outside. It shouldn't be just a transaction; that is not in the spirit of the product. So we help manage the buying process, the experience of drinking, and the pathway and rhythm the customer experiences from one purchase to the next. And pricing is a part of that pathway.

She showed me a few of the emails:

> You should just sell a good product at a good price. Stop manipulating people.

> People can decide for themselves what experience they want from a product – maybe if you didn't waste time on

trying to figure that out for them, you could sell your teapots at a sensible price.

Ethics

These emails raise a valid question. Is it our place as suppliers to try to understand how our customers think and feel? Or should we just offer products and let them worry about that? And if we do understand how they feel, is it OK for us to take advantage of that to lead them to pay us more money?

Each person has their own ethical position, and I can't tell you for sure what to do. But I can suggest some approaches that may help illuminate the questions for you and help you make your own decision. There are several ways to think about these points, based on both practice and principle.

One is from a scientific understanding of how people make buying decisions. People really are influenced by how they feel. They are influenced by what they assume a price signifies. There is no way to create an 'objective' buying decision that is based on purely rational considerations. And so a supplier has no choice but to try to understand the psychology of their consumer and work with it.

If you try to act *as if* people buy your products rationally, it won't magically come true. They will still be irrational, and your price signals will be interpreted in a way that might bear no relation to the facts about the benefits and quality of your product.

Another answer is based on competitive market considerations. If your competitors use pricing psychology and you don't, you will eventually go out of business. In the long run, that will make the market less competitive and provide no benefit at all to your customers. Indeed, with less competition in the market they will be worse off after you're gone.

In some cases, your pricing tactics are simply intended to bring people back to a more rational way of making decisions – by lowering the cognitive barriers that consumers put up when they don't trust their supplier. The example in Chapter 16 on 'other people's money' shows how the pricing proposition was carefully designed to reduce barriers to purchase, and to make clear that the benefits to the client outweighed the costs.

Finally, remember that customers – as a whole – are out for the best deal they can get. They won't hesitate to take advantage tactically of promotions, sales and the like in order to get the best possible deal from you and other suppliers. You don't owe them anything – at least, you owe them a decent quality service and you owe it to them not to mislead them – but you don't have to be generous.

The law

The legal aspects are reasonably clear. Please note that the following is not legal advice and if you have any questions about your particular situation, your own solicitor should be able to help answer them.

The Office of Fair Trading (in the UK) regulates businesses, and one of the principles of the law is that commercial practices must not be misleading. This is backed up by European law, but the principles of law are interpreted slightly differently in each country.

In 2010 the OFT released a report called *Advertising of Prices*, which is available at www.oft.gov.uk.

The study carried out for this report investigated five key pricing practices in order to determine whether they could be considered misleading to customers.

The results were in line with existing regulation, which requires that, for example, a sale price which is compared to a reference price – 'Was £50, now £20' – must be an honest representation of the previous price. You can't just make up the £50 price, and you might get into trouble if you sold the product at £50 for only one day four months ago in your Inverness branch.

'Drip pricing' was a particular focus of the study. This is where an advertised price turns out not to be genuine, because there are a lot of mandatory additional items. The best-known example of this is from the airline industry. Some airlines (notably Ryanair) used to advertise tickets at £5, 99p or even free; but when customers visited the website to buy them, they would discover that there were a number of mandatory additional fees – airport fees, taxes and so on. The actual price usually turned out to be £40 or more. Notionally, customers could then make an informed choice whether to buy the product, having now discovered the correct price. However, because they had already made an investment of time in getting through the website to this point, many customers decided to go ahead and buy the ticket anyway, instead of going to check other airline sites and compare their prices. The OFT considers this pricing practice to be misleading and has warned companies not to use it.

In any case, most businesses care about how their customers see them. Pricing practices which approach the border between what's legal and what is not, or practices based on misleading customers, are likely to lead to a backlash. I therefore recommend that you avoid using any misleading price communications or drip-pricing approaches, and stick to the techniques recommended in this book.

Chapter summary

- In the UK, pricing is rarely directly regulated but falls within the general laws on commercial practices.

- It is important not to mislead customers with your price communication.

- Customers are just as keen as you are to get a good deal. They are happy to play one supplier off against another, so it's not unreasonable to play the same games against them.

Epilogue

Two years later: how Maggie fought the investment bankers and what happened next

As I left the factory one afternoon Maggie said she might not be able to see me for a while. "Some people" were apparently sensitive about the book, and didn't want their details to become public. She promised to fill me in on everything later, "after everything is completed".

I guess she did plan it all, then – or at least she wanted me to think so. I'm still not sure what to believe. Looking back, though, it's clear that Maggie realised that all the techniques she had developed to use with consumers could also be used on corporate executives. She was now ready to negotiate.

In any case, the next time I arrived for a session I couldn't get into her office. She was locked away in meetings that day, and the next, and the next week when I came back again. The head of PR, whom the company had now got round to hiring, was helpful with facts in an official kind of way, but he wouldn't – or couldn't – say what was going on behind closed doors. Once I caught a glimpse of four people in dark suits leaving the building, but nobody was talking.

My story in this chapter is pieced together from what I could infer from third parties, dropped clues and snatches of conversation. Eventually I did get confirmation of some of these facts from Maggie. But they must be interpreted cautiously.

It seems that there had been some corporate moves in the consumer goods world. Maybe you read about them in the FT. Global consumer products company Leverkraft & Gamble had taken over Cosanostra Coffee as part of a strategy of acquiring higher-margin businesses and building a closer relationship with their consumers. When the Chocolate Teapot Company's sales through the major supermarkets had reached five million units, Valerie Salmon, now promoted to vice-president of Leverkraft & Gamble, gave Maggie a call.

"We keep an eye on fast-growing suppliers in the food and drink sector," she explained. "Would you be interested in talking – no particular agenda, just to see what sort of relationship we could develop?"

To Maggie, this was clearly code for "You're a competitor now – we want to buy you or get rid of you." So she suggested Salmon pay a visit – and made a few other calls too.

When Salmon arrived she was left in the reception to wait, and saw her counterpart from another of the major consumer goods firms leaving Maggie's office before her. I am sure this could have been no accident. What she didn't see was the investment bank adviser who sat in the next room listening in.

When Salmon was invited into the office, Maggie laid down three conditions before she would enter into negotiations on a relationship.

First, any acquisition must be on a multiple of at least 24 times annual profits. This demand was designed to anchor the buyer to a high value, even if she only expected to get a multiple of 20 in reality.

Second, it should be structured for a payout over four years, using hyperbolic discounting to reduce current resistance to payment; after all, there was a good chance that the executive making the acquisition might not be in the same job four years later.

Third, the payout should be 80% in equity and adjusted for stock price increases in the meantime. This condition made the purchase feel less expensive because it removes most of the cash element, which is much more salient than a purchase based on shares. It also has the advantage that the acquiring company itself does not have to pay directly for the purchase; instead, its shareholders implicitly pay through the dilution of their shares. Structures like this are often much easier for executives to stomach than anything which directly hits the financial results their bonuses are based on.

Salmon couldn't, of course, know what – if anything – her competitors had agreed to, but apparently decided it could do no harm to note Maggie's requests and continue the conversation. She noted the caveat that any offer would have to be agreed by the board. Maybe her intention was to negotiate downwards later, or walk away from the deal if necessary, but the door was now open to an agreement.

Then Maggie shifted the premise of the conversation. In fact, she said, the real reason we should be talking is not about chocolate teapots. It's because we have built this business using a completely new approach to designing prices and product ranges. If you buy us, you have the opportunity to use these techniques across all your other products. She pointed out that the net profit achieved by the Chocolate Teapot Company was nearly 60% of revenue – about four times the average level achieved by Salmon's employer on their food range.

Salmon agreed that this could be a factor in her company's reasons for wanting to work with Maggie. At this point Maggie started to put in place the pieces of a possible deal.

"Let me run a repackaging trial – I will talk to a few of your product managers and work with them to design a new pricing strategy for some of your products. Whatever net profit increase I can achieve, you can keep 75% of it and I'll take 25%. Can I talk to your pricing people and see who's interested in working with me?"

Salmon may not have been wild about this idea but, with her competitors walking in and out of the same building, she wanted to keep Maggie interested. A conditional profit share wouldn't be too harmful. And what harm could it do to let her talk to a few of Salmon's colleagues?

Well, Maggie is a persuasive woman. The next week when she spoke to the company's product and pricing managers they *liked what she had to offer. She was ready to put some power in their hands – power that had always previously been with the finance and operations people in Leverkraft – and some real rewards. Her offer was accepted almost unanimously across Leverkraft's 600 pricing managers.*

Maggie swiftly deployed all the tools she'd developed at the Chocolate Teapot Company. In every product category she encouraged the product and marketing managers to examine the emotional and material values of their consumers, and to develop a model of the competitive environment and existing product price anchors. She showed them how to invent new product options by reframing the product to disrupt existing anchor points, and how to persuade consumers to pay more by deferring payments into the future. They developed new bundles and launched their new products through a range of different channels. There was a new energy at Leverkraft, and suddenly the industry started to notice that new ideas were emerging from one of the big groups for once, not the upstarts.

You may have seen the resulting change in the consumer products market over the last two years. Maggie has called it the "cognitive revolution". Consumers are not just making choices between commodity products any more. They enter into a relationship with a retailer, a brand and a series of consumption environments, where their cognitive benefits are as much part of the outcome as the physical benefits of consuming the products.

Perhaps you have tried the new Washing Powder Subscription Service that was launched last year, or the high-priced Energy Vodka Yoghurt products now being sold in nightclubs around the country. No doubt you will be familiar with the Bling Nappies range made famous by Brad and Angelina's new adopted baby, and the new consultancy that Leverkraft & Gamble is offering, helping large companies improve staff productivity by laying on a range of personalised consumer products for them in the workplace. There's even a partnership with a well-known search engine, which is giving away free chocolate bars for the first 50 people to find a secret search engine keyword every day.

Of course, these new consumer relationships come with more opportunities to create value for the customer as well as to make money. Leverkraft has managed for the first time to establish its corporate brand alongside its product brands in many consumers' minds. As a result of these innovations, Leverkraft has changed the competitive dynamic of the industry. The stable and comfortable equilibrium that had prevailed for decades was disrupted. Maggie's schemes increased the company's profit margin in two years from 8% to 18% – especially impressive on a worldwide turnover of £75bn, translating to an increase in pre-tax profits from £6bn to £14bn. Of that £8bn increase, the Chocolate Teapot Company collected £2bn in profit share.

This was far beyond what anyone had expected – the value of Leverkraft shares soared, making its management rich and its shareholders happy. Maggie had written her deal in advance, and the acquisition had been agreed on a multiple of 20 times profits.

It was at that moment she managed to get Leverkraft to complete its acquisition of CTC. The transaction was timed perfectly. Based on 20 times £2bn, and her holding converted to equity in the parent company, Maggie ended up owning over 20% of Leverkraft & Gamble's stock.

The competitors have started fighting back with their own pricing schemes, and the profits may not last. But the new company – now renamed CTC Group – has established itself as the undisputed industry leader in a way they had never managed before. The annual shareholders' meeting came round just a few weeks ago, with Maggie hailed in industry magazines as the visionary figure of the sector. The meeting was expected to nominate her as CEO. Shareholders eagerly awaited the announcement of the next step in her vision for pricing, for branding, for distribution – whatever the next shakeup in the sector was going to be.

The anticipation made it all the more shocking when she did not show up. Perhaps you saw her message on the news, announcing her resignation from the board and nominating her replacement, the previously out-of-favour vice-president Valerie Salmon. You might have noticed that Sir Charles Leverkraft was unceremoniously fired from his position as CEO – though you might not have known that his investment company CLH Property was the one that evicted Maggie's parents from their shop several years ago. You may have speculated with the rest of us about the foundation into which her shares were placed, what its plans are, and who might be in charge of it. Maggie hasn't been in touch with the company since that message and neither they nor I know where she is. And yet – I can't imagine that we've heard the last from her.

Pricing and your business

Maybe this outcome is not what you want for your business. You might prefer simply to increase your margins and not worry about revolutionising your whole industry. That's fine. In either case, this book has shown you how to do it.

In Chapter 1, we looked at how to use pricing as a positioning tool, especially when launching new products or services, although this is also a fundamental question for your existing products too.

In Chapter 2 we looked at the baseline cost to give you a floor under your prices and to examine one of the factors that sophisticated customers may consider in their decision about how much to pay you.

In Chapter 3 we showed how to estimate what your customers are really willing to pay for what you offer, and how to differentiate your product versions to capture maximum revenue from each customer class.

In Chapter 4 we examined customer segmentation, how to ask questions that will uncover the truth from consumers, and how to make your pricing fit each group of customers and their perceptions of your product's or service's value.

Chapter 5 examined how introducing a new product may need both self-belief and belief by third parties in your pricing power. It showed how to communicate your evidence confidently in such a way that your partners or resellers will believe in it.

In Chapter 6 we launched the new product and discovered the power of first impressions and the difficulty of changing a consumer's mind, along with some techniques for doing so.

Chapter 7 introduced the power of anchoring, showing how high prices can create a value perception in the mind of a consumer with only a vague idea of how much to pay for your product or service.

Chapter 8 discussed competition and what to do when people try to undercut you – or how to successfully attack other companies with an aggressive pricing strategy.

In Chapter 9 we saw the power of decoys, which can take the form of either a feature price decoy or a pure price decoy, and in both cases can affect consumer behaviour in your favour.

Chapter 10 showed how to use hyperbolic discounting to get consumers to pay more for your product by paying for it in the future.

Chapter 11 examined two topics: social and peer effects on willingness to pay; and the endowment effect and loss aversion. These can be difficult to apply so we looked at mechanisms to introduce them into the sales process for your product or service.

In Chapter 12 we designed bundles to increase the perceived value of your products and make them harder to compare on price with the competition.

In Chapter 13 we looked at the power of 'free' as a price point. Free offers can attract new customers or increase willingness to pay for non-free products.

Chapter 14 showed how to upsell customers with add-on items or more expensive versions of the same product.

Chapter 15 examined how to change the perception of your price by attaching it to something larger; and, similarly, to show that your price is great value by basing it directly on the value or profit that the customer gets from buying.

Chapter 16 discussed how price perception works when the customer is spending someone else's money rather than their own, and how the ability to rationalise a price becomes as important as true value.

Chapter 17 examined the complexities of the pricing environment and the risks that different techniques can conflict when used in different sales channels. It looked at how memory, brand consistency and channel differentiation can help you stay consistent and defend against price arbitrage.

In Chapter 18 we focused on charitable giving, both as a sales technique and because of what it reveals about the psychology of how we purchase products in general.

Finally, Chapter 19 considered the legal and ethical aspects of pricing and the importance of not misleading customers.

Together, this suite of techniques and psychological discoveries provides a comprehensive approach to setting the pricing strategy for new or existing services or products. As we saw in this epilogue, the same approaches can be used on investment decisions such as selling your company, as well as in consumer and business pricing.

You may wish to increase the profits of your company using a new pricing strategy in order to expand, to sell the business, or simply to be able to take home more money and spend it on yourself. Whichever it is, pricing is your main tool for increasing the perceived value you create for customers and keeping a decent share of it in return.

I received a letter last week with an illegible postmark and an airmail sticker. It was unsigned, but the handwriting was familiar, and I had already guessed who it had come from. She won't mind if I share the last paragraph with you.

Prices, for all their significance, are just one of the messages we send each other when we trade and work together. This particular message relates to something people care a lot about – the amount of money in their pocket – so people treat it as important. Prices are just one part of the economic conversation, but they reveal deeper values at work. A price is a simple way for us to make a decision that trades off between things that are too important for us to compare directly. A price may just look like a number. But until we all figure out what we really care about in this rich, subtle and complicated system called the economy, prices will be the language we speak. Treat them with care – they reveal your true feelings.

Bibliography and further reading

The following are useful general sources for information and ideas on pricing, both theory and practice.

Willam Poundstone's *Priceless: The Hidden Psychology of Value* (Hill & Wang/Oneworld, 2010) is a very good collection for general readers of different pricing anecdotes and approaches, and describes many of the original experiments in which these approaches were discovered.

Smart Pricing by Wharton professors Jagmohan Raju and Z. John Zhang (Pearson Prentice Hall, 2010) illustrates a smaller range of practical approaches to pricing than *Priceless*, but does so in more detail.

The Marketing Science Institute in 2006 published *Pricing* by Russell Winer, which contains a solid and comprehensive review of most market research techniques to have been written up in academic literature.

A number of good books on pricing exist which do not focus on psychology. For example Baker, Marn and Zawada's *The Price Advantage* (John Wiley & Sons, 2010) and Reed Holden's *Pricing With Confidence* (John Wiley & Sons, 2008).

There are a number of technical books on the economic theory of pricing, such as Milton Friedman's *Price Theory* (most recent edition by Transaction Publishers, 2007) or Steven E. Landsburg's *Price Theory and Applications* (Cengage Learning, 2008). These focus on the traditional theory of suppy and demand, and do not engage in pricing psychology at all. Similarly, *How to Price* by Oz Shy (Cambridge University Press, 2008) gives an overview of methods that are do not take a psychological approach, but are instead based on traditional (rational) economics.

Several books on behavioural economics cover some of the pricing techniques outlined here. *Basic Instincts* by Peter Lunn (Marshall Cavendish, 2010) is one of the best; *Predictably Irrational* by Dan Ariely (HarperCollins, 2008) and *Nudge* by Richard H. Thaler and Cass R. Sunstein (Yale University Press, 2008) are also good. All three cover a whole range of behavioural phenomena and biases that go beyond the pricing world.

The methods and techniques described in each chapter are not necessarily directly based on the publications referenced below, but the articles will provide more insight and a broader understanding of the approaches from each chapter.

Chapter 1: Pricing as positioning

- Dobson, Gregory and Shlomo Kalish (1988): 'Positioning and pricing a product line'. *Marketing Science*, Vol 7 no 2.

- Hauser, John R. (1988): 'Competitive price and positioning strategies'. *Marketing Science*, Vol 7 no 1.

- Lewis, R. C. (1981): 'The positioning statement for hotels'. *The Cornell Hotel and Restaurant Administrative Quarterly*, Vol 22(1), 51–61.

- Nagle, T. T. (1987): *The Strategy and Tactics of Pricing: A Guide to Profitable Decision Making*. Prentice Hall.

- Shaw, Margaret (1992): 'Positioning and price: merging theory, strategy and tactics'. *Journal of Hospitality & Tourism Research*, Vol 15, no 2, p 31.

Chapter 2: Cost-based calculations

Most business economics textbooks – and even some accountancy books – will expand on the basic principles presented in this chapter. For example:

- Harris, Neil (2012): *Business Economics: Theory and Application*. Routledge.

- Thomas, Christopher R. and S. Charles Maurice (2010): *Managerial Economics*. McGraw-Hill.

There are plenty of more academic treatments of the dynamics of cost-based pricing. Two examples are:

- Maskin, E. and J. Tirole (1988): 'A theory of dynamic oligopoly II: price competition, kinked demand curves and Edgeworth cycles'. *Econometrica*, Vol 56.

- Noel, Michael (2003): 'Edgeworth price cycles, cost-based pricing and sticky pricing in retail gasoline markets'. Department of Economics, UC San Diego.

Chapter 3: Reading the customer's mind

- Phlips, Louis (1983): *The Economics of Price Discrimination*. Cambridge University Press.

- Rao, Vithala R. (ed) (2009): *Handbook of Pricing Research in Marketing*. Edward Elgar Publishing.

- Winer, Russell S. (2006): *Pricing*. Marketing Science Institute.

Chapter 4: Segmentation

- Kotler, Philip and Kevin Lane Keller (2006): *Marketing Management*. Pearson Prentice Hall.

- Pigou, Arthur Cecil (1952). *Economics of Welfare*. Transaction Publishers.

- Stiving, Mark (2011): *Impact Pricing*. Entrepreneur Press.

In focus: does 99p pricing work?

- See refs in *Priceless*

Chapter 5: New launches, belief and fairness

- Bolton, L. E., L. Warlop and J. W. Alba (2003): 'Consumer perceptions of price (un)fairness'. *Journal of Consumer Research*, Vol 29 part 4.

- Huang, Jen-Hung, Ching-Te Chang and Cathy Yi-Hsuan Chen (2005): 'Perceived fairness of pricing on the Internet'. *Journal of Economic Psychology*, Vol 26 issue 3.

- Hultink, Erik Jan, Susan Hart, Henry S. J. Robben and Abbie Griffin (2000): 'Launch decisions and new product success'. *Journal of Product Innovation Management*, Vol 17 issue 1.

- Maxwell, Sarah (2008): *The Price Is Wrong*. John Wiley & Sons.

- Shehryar, Omar and David M. Hunt (2005): 'Buyer behavior and procedural fairness in pricing: exploring the moderating role of product familiarity'. *Journal of Product and Brand Management*, Vol 14 issue 4.

- Zeithaml, Valarie A. (1988): 'Consumer perceptions of price, quality and value'. *The Journal of Marketing*.

Chapter 6: Memory and expectations, trials and reframing your prices

- Cestari, Vincenzo, Paolo del Giovane and Clelia Rossi-Arnaud (2007): 'Memory for prices and the Euro cash changeover: an analysis for cinema prices in Italy'. *Bank of Italy Economic Research Paper*, No. 619.

- Diamond, William D. and Leland Campbell (1989): 'The framing of sales promotions: effects on reference price change'. *Advances in Consumer Research*, Vol 16.

- Goering, Patricia A. (1985): 'Effects of product trial on consumer expectations, demand and prices'. *Journal of Consumer Research*, Vol 12 issue 1.

- Gourville, J. T. (1998): 'Pennies-a-day: the effect of temporal reframing on transaction evaluation'. *Journal of Consumer Research*, Vol 24 no 4.

- Mazumdar, Tridib and Purushottam Papatla (1995): 'Loyalty differences in the use of internal and external reference prices'. *Marketing Letters*, Vol 6 no 2.

■ Winer, Russell S. (1986): 'A reference price model of brand choice'. *Journal of Consumer Research*, Vol 13.

Chapter 7: Anchoring

■ Chapman, Gretchen B. and Eric J. Johnson (1999): 'Anchoring, activation and the construction of values'. *Organizational Behavior and Human Decision Processes*, Vol 79 issue 2.

■ Epley, Nicholas and Thomas Gilovich (2006): 'The anchoring-and-adjustment heuristic: why the adjustments are insufficient'. *Psychological Science*, Vol 17 no 4.

■ Slovic, Paul and Sarah Lichtenstein (1983): 'Preference reversals: a broader perspective'. *The American Economic Review*, Vol 73 issue 4.

■ Yadav, M. S. (1994): 'How buyers evaluate product bundles: A model of anchoring and adjustment'. *Journal of Consumer Research*, Vol 21 no 2.

Chapter 8: Competition

■ Cotterill, Ronald W., William P. Putsis, Jr. and Ravi Dhar (2000): 'Assessing the competitive interaction between private labels and national brands'. *The Journal of Business*, Vol 73 no 1.

■ Coughlan, Anne T. and Murali K. Mantrala (1992): 'Dynamic competitive pricing strategies'. *International Journal of Research in Marketing*, Vol 9 issue 1.

■ Dickson, Peter R. (1992): 'Towards a general theory of competitive rationality'. *The Journal of Marketing*, Vol 56(1).

- Gabaix, Xavier and David Laibson (2005): 'Shrouded attributes, consumer myopia and information suppression in competitive markets'. *NBER Working Paper*, No. 11755.

- Gerla, Harry S. (1985): 'The psychology of predatory pricing: why predatory pricing pays'. *Southwestern Law Journal*, Vol 39(3), p 755.

- Kopalle, Praveen et al (2009): 'Retailer pricing and competitive effects'. *Journal of Retailing*, Vol 85 issue 1.

Chapter 9: Decoys

- Ariely, Dan and Thomas S. Wallsten (1995): 'Seeking subjective dominance in multidimensional space: an explanation of the asymmetric dominance effect'. *Organizational Behavior and Human Decision Processes*, Vol 63 issue 3.

- Bateman, Ian J., Alistair Munro and Gregory L. Poe (2008): 'Decoy effects in choice experiments and contingent valuation: asymmetric dominance'. *Land Economics*, Vol 84 no 1.

- Munro, Alistair and Robert Sugden (2003): 'On the theory of reference-dependent preferences'. *Journal of Economic Behavior & Organization*, Vol 50 issue 4.

- Simonson, Itamar and Amos Tversky (1992): 'Choice in context: trade off contrast and extremeness aversion'. *Journal of Marketing Research*, Vol 29(3).

Chapter 10: Paying tomorrow for what you get today

■ Dasgupta, P. and E. Maskin (2005): 'Uncertainty and hyperbolic discounting'. *American Economic Review*, Vol 95 no 4.

■ Laibson, David (1997): 'Golden eggs and hyperbolic discounting'. *The Quarterly Journal of Economics*, Vol 112(2).

■ Liberman, Nira, Yaacov Trope and Elena Stephan (2007): 'Psychological distance'. *Social Psychology: Handbook of Basic Principles* (eds. Kruglanski and Higgins), Guilford Press.

■ Onwujekwe, Obinna et al (2001): 'Hypothetical and actual willingness-to-pay for insecticide-treated nets in five Nigerian communities'. *Tropical Medicine and International Health*, Vol 6 issue 7.

■ Rubinstein, Ariel (2003): ' "Economics and Psychology"? The case of hyperbolic discounting'. *International Economic Review*, Vol 44 issue 4.

■ Trope, Yaacov, Nira Liberman and Cheryl Wakslak (2007): 'Construal levels and psychological distance: effects on representation, prediction, evaluation and behaviour'. *Journal of Consumer Psychology*, Vol 17(2).

Chapter 11: The tea party

■ Amaldoss, Wilfred and Sanjay Jain (2005): 'Pricing of conspicuous goods: a competitive analysis of social effects'. *Journal of Marketing Research*, Vol 42 no 1.

- Kahneman, Daniel, Jack L. Knetsch and Richard H. Thaler (1991): 'Anomalies: the endowment effect, loss aversion and status quo bias'. *The Journal of Economic Perspectives*, Vol 5 issue 1.

- Loewenstein, George F., Leigh Thompson and Max H. Bazerman (1989): 'Social utility and decision-making in interpersonal contexts'. *Journal of Personality and Social Psychology*, Vol 57(3).

- Monroe, Kent B. (1973): 'Buyers' subjective perceptions of price'. *Journal of Marketing Research*, Vol 10(1).

- Moretti, Enrico (2011): 'Social learning and peer effects in consumption: evidence from movie sales'. *Review of Economic Studies*, Vol 78(1).

- Jacoby, Jacob, Jerry C. Olson and Rafael A. Haddock (1971): 'Price, brand name and product composition characteristics as determinants of perceived quality'. *Journal of Applied Psychology*, Vol 55(6).

Chapter 12: Bundling

- Adams, William James and Janet L. Yellen (1976): 'Commodity bundling and the burden of monopoly'. *Quarterly Journal of Economics*, Vol 90.

- Hanson, Ward and R. Kipp Martin (1990): 'Optimal bundle pricing'. *Management Science*, Vol 36 issue 2.

- Kaicker, Ajit, William O. Bearden and Kenneth C. Manning (1995): 'Component versus bundle pricing: the role of selling price deviations from price expectations'. *Journal of Business Research*, Vol 33 issue 3.

- Olderog, Torsten and Bernd Skiera (2000): 'The benefits of bundling strategies'. *Schmalenbach Business Review*, Vol 52

Chapter 13: Free offers

- Ariely, Dan (2008): *Predictably Irrational: The Hidden Forces that Shape our Decisions*, chapter 3. HarperCollins.

- Nunes, Joseph C. and Xavier Dreze (2006): 'The endowed progress effect: how artificial advancement increases effort'. *Journal of Consumer Research*, Vol 32 no 4.

- Ries, Al and Jack Trout (1994): *The 22 Immutable Laws of Marketing*. Harper Business.

Chapter 14: Upselling

- Aydin, Goker and Serhan Ziya (2008): 'Pricing promotional products under upselling'. *Manufacturing & Service Operations Management*, Vol 10 no 3.

- Chapman, G. B. and B. H. Bornstein (1996): 'The more you ask for, the more you get: anchoring in personal injury verdicts'. *Applied Cognitive Psychology*, Vol 10 no 6.

While there is not an extensive treatment of upselling in the academic literature, there are a number of popular books that deal with it, such as:

- Schiffman, Stefan (2005): *Upselling Techniques: That Really Work!* Adams Media.

Chapter 15: Absorption and value pricing

- Kortge, G. Dean and Patrick A. Okonkwo (1993): 'Perceived value approach to pricing'. *Industrial Marketing Management*, Vol 22 issue 2.

Ron Baker has written a number of books on value pricing, such as *Implementing Value Pricing* (John Wiley & Sons, 2010) and *Pricing for Value* (SPCK Publishing, 1999) – primarily aimed at those in professional services such as lawyers or accountants.

The term **absorption pricing** is used in a different sense in some of the literature, to refer to a cost-based pricing method. The sense I use it in this chapter is that the psychological decision to buy a smaller product is **absorbed** into a bigger decision and therefore becomes easier.

Chapter 16: Other people's money

The principal-agent problem is covered in most intermediate economics textbooks and many journal articles, for example:

- Grossman, Sanford J. and Oliver D. Hart (1983): 'An analysis of the principal-agent problem'. *Econometrica*, Vol 51 no 1.

- Laffont, Jean-Jacques and David Martimort (2001): *The Theory of Incentives: The Principal-Agent Model*. Princeton University Press.

There is an even bigger literature on business-to-business sales more generally. You could start with:

- Boaz, Nate, John Murnane and Kevin Nuffer (2010): 'The basics of business-to-business sales success'. *McKinsey*

Quarterly, May 2010. Accessible at: www.
mckinseyquarterly.com/The_basics_of_business-to-
business_sales_success_2586

■ Coe, John (2003): *The Fundamentals of Business-to-Business Sales and Marketing*. McGraw-Hill Professional.

Chapter 17: Managing the pricing environment

■ Kopalle, Praveen K., Ambar G. Rao and João L. Assunção (1996): 'Asymmetric reference price effects and dynamic pricing policies'. *Marketing Science*, Vol 15 no 1.

■ Shipley, David and Elizabeth Bourdon (1990): 'Distributor pricing in very competitive markets'. *Industrial Marketing Management*, Vol 19 issue 3.

Chapter 18: The psychology of giving

This is another field with its own in-depth literature. If you are interested I suggest starting with the following collection of papers, from which you can start an exploration of the broader literature on the subject.

■ Oppenheimer, Daniel M. and Christopher Y. Olivola (eds.) (2010): *The Science of Giving: Experimental Approaches to the Study of Charity*. Psychology Press.

Chapter 19: The ethics and law of pricing

Pricing law varies according to the jurisdiction you are in. UK readers can find some useful information at Business link (www.gov.uk/uk-welcomes-business)

As this book is aimed at the United Kingdom, I have not reviewed the legal situation in other countries – however for the US, you could start with the guide at National Institute of Standards and Technology (www.nist.gov)

There is also some treatment of pricing law in:

- Baker, Walter L., Michael V. Marn and Craig C. Zawada (2010): 'Legal degrees of freedom'. *The Price Advantage*, chapter 9. John Wiley & Sons.

The ethics of pricing have not been explored extensively but there is a growing literature on ethics in behavioural economics more generally, for example:

- Bovens, Luc (2009): 'The ethics of nudge'. *Preference Change. Theory and Decision Library A*, Vol 42. Springer.

- Selinger, Evan and Kyle Whyte: 'Is there a right way to nudge: the practice and ethics of choice architecture'. *Sociology Compass*, Vol 5 issue 10.

However these mainly focus on the issues for public policymakers – the ethics of behavioural economics in business is yet to develop as a discipline.

Appendix A

A pricing diagnostic

Now that you are familiar with the most powerful pricing techniques, you can run this quick diagnostic exercise on your own business. These questions will help you figure out how close your current pricing policy is to the optimal strategy.

30 questions to ask to find out if your pricing is optimal

1. What alternative products or services do customers compare you with when they consider purchasing from you?

2. How does your pricing compare with the competition?

3. What are your gross margins on different products?

4. If a customer is willing to pay more than you're charging, what tactics do you have for capturing their extra budget?

5. What attributes does a customer really want when they buy each of your products?

6. How many options do you give a customer when they are looking at buying from you?

7. What do you do for customers who want your product, can't quite afford it now but will have more money next month or next quarter?

8. What do you give away for free?

9. What have you done to 'blind' your products – to make them hard to compare directly with competitive options?

10. What decoys are available to customers to make your products more attractive?

11. What experiments have you done to measure or test your market's willingness to pay?

12. Which customers have you chosen not to sell to?

13. Do you offer both a product and service version of what you sell?

14. Do you make the intangible tangible?

15. When and how will you next reframe your offering to increase price?

16. What more expensive purchases do you attach your products to, to reduce price resistance?

17. How do you use anchoring to increase the perception of the value of your products?

18. What bundles do you offer with your products, to make them harder to compare with alternatives?

19. Who do you consider your closest competitors?

20. What do you do to defend against their pricing strategies?

21. Do you know what price, or what pricing model, your customers think is fair?

22. What are you doing to shift their view of fairness, and demonstrate that you have the right to charge more?

23. What is the total value of what you provide to clients?

24. What do your clients *think* the total value is? How are you demonstrating to them that your true value is higher?

25. How do you upsell clients once they have bought one product from you?

26. Through which channels do you sell? What others could you sell through?

27. What are the objectives of the other businesses (and people) in your channels?

28. What constraints do they operate under?

29. Do customers have the chance to buy from you with someone else's money?

30. How do you use pricing to create a regular purchase habit?

A quick-reference method for pricing a new product

This step-by-step questionnaire will clarify the key pricing questions and strategies available to you.

1. What benefits do your clients get from your product or service? List these in the benefit matrix in Chapter 1. We will refer to these as *values*. Think as broadly as you can – the examples provided in that chapter will help you see the kind of emotional and intangible values that are often at play alongside the more obvious ones.

2. What other products or services do they get similar benefits from? List them alongside the values in the table at the end of Chapter 1.

3. What units do these come in? Try to come up with a quantity which matches the most common single purchase size of your product. For example, if you sell a head massage product which is effective against headaches, work out how many painkillers a customer would need to use over the lifetime of your product to get the equivalent benefit. Or if you sell train tickets, work out for what length of time a person would need to own a car to travel the equivalent distance.

4. How much do they pay for those products? Write down a range under 'Price per unit'. If you're using painkillers as an example, write down the generic price as well as the price for the leading brand. Remember to translate this price into the same units that you used in the 'Units of value' column.

5. Now you must be ruthless with yourself. Ignore all but three of the benefits. Your customers cannot focus on

dozens of benefits all at once; therefore you need to choose which ones you are going to talk to them about. The most valuable benefits are probably those with the highest comparison price. The benefits you choose are called the **critical value dimensions**.

6. Write down the three critical value dimensions. You now need to analyse how your customers seek out and choose a product when they have a need in those dimensions. For example, if the critical value dimension is 'pain relief', ask yourself how your customers go about achieving pain relief. It may be to go to the cupboard and see if there are any aspirin left. It may be to go to the chemist and buy some more. It may be to take a bath or lie down in a darkened room. You are writing down the customer's **solution strategy** for the particular need that you help them with.

7. What do you think is the pricing conversation that goes on in the customer's head when carrying out this solution strategy. What do they think about the price they expect to pay to solve this problem? What's a solution worth to them? You first want to focus on the higher end of the price range: for example, what is it that a customer thinks when they are choosing to buy Nurofen Plus as opposed to generic ibuprofen?

8. Your job is to construct an argument linking all three critical value dimensions, and add together the alternative price for each. You should now have an idea of the target price for your product. This is **the highest price that a customer will pay for an alternative solution to the same problem**. Write this down.

9. Now it is time to apply the psychological pricing techniques that will let you achieve this price. Start with Chapter 5 and, briefly visiting each chapter, consider whether you can use the techniques. The checklist between Chapters 18 and 19 may also be helpful.

Appendix B

A theory of psychology and cognition: the background to this book

This section of the book should be considered optional. Many readers will be happy to know how to apply the advice in the main body of the book without reading the theory behind it. However, if you know more, you'll be able to understand how pricing psychology works and perhaps design your own techniques.

This overview combines insights from biology, psychology, cognitive science and behavioural economics. You won't find it replicated exactly in any textbook, but it's all drawn from recent empirical and theoretical research in those fields.

All theories of psychology, economics and human behaviour share some basic features. They study people and ask what makes those people act the way they do. Broadly, people try to make their experience of the world better, and they make choices in accordance with that objective.

Traditional economists view these choices in a particular way. They consider the person's experience of the world to be summarised in a variable called **utility**: the higher the utility, the happier the person is. At all times, people make the choices that result in the highest possible utility. Economists also tend to focus only on material choices – we achieve utility by buying or selling goods or services. And the key question in economics is: how much of one good do we exchange for another? That is, what is the price of each good? Economics is the study of how we exchange goods and services at certain prices to make ourselves happier.

Psychologists mostly study behaviour at a lower level. They look at the way people respond to an external stimulus, how that affects the state of their brain, and what actions they take as a result. They examine some basic mental variables to see how they affect these processes.

- Emotion – how does emotion affect the way we view the world or the actions we take?

- Attention – if we are focused on a particular stimulus, can we still notice what else is happening or think about something else?

- Learning – how quickly or reliably can we remember past experiences and use them to our advantage?

Neither of these approaches is wrong, but they both expose only a part of the picture. To understand enough about human behaviour to set prices accurately, you need to know how to use both approaches and more besides.

The problem with traditional economics is that it paints too simple a picture – the idea that people maximise utility is elegant but crude. This simplicity enables economists to study how a whole population of people and goods fit together, but it means that some of the results they get are wrong. The problem with using traditional psychology in business is the opposite – it is too complicated. Psychological research covers too many different details, many of which you cannot measure or control in a business environment, and if you try to incorporate every one of them you will have too many permutations to deal with.

The cognitive theory that I lay out here strikes a balance between these two extremes. It takes into account some of the key psychological effects that are omitted from traditional economics, but puts them into a simple enough model to enable it to be practically useful for setting your prices. I call it 'cognitive economics' and it is a powerful tool for understanding how consumers really make a decision about buying your product and spending money on it.

We start with the individual consumer. At any moment, they have some awareness of the world around them – an incomplete, imperfect awareness, but as valid as anyone else's. This awareness includes both the outside world – the place in which they are physically located, the things they can see and hear, the people near them, the products they could buy – and the internal world, their feelings, desires and wants.

The consumer always perceives some lack or deficit in the world. Technically, there may be moments when they think everything is perfect and nothing could be improved. But at those times, they will not take any actions. The only thing that can drive a person to act is the desire to make the world better in some way. This lack need not be an absolute lack, in the sense that something is missing; it could be an opportunity to improve something, for instance to earn some money. It's a gap between how the world could be, and how it is.

How we interpret the world and determine the lack is a function of our biology, combined with the relationships we have learned throughout our lives between external lacks and internal needs. The most basic lacks are straightforward physical needs – when we are hungry, tired, thirsty, in pain or horny our body informs our brain of that fact by releasing chemicals or sending nerve signals. Built on top of these are aspects of the external world – a lack of money, or the knowledge that the fridge is empty and we might want to eat later, or the belief that a good film is on at the cinema and we are currently missing out. And sometimes it is an interim lack, which we become aware of while we satisfy some other need. For example, to earn money we may decide to get a job; having done so, a new series of lacks will drive our behaviour, such as the knowledge that we have been assigned a task and it is not finished yet.

We are continually learning about lacks in the world and new ways to address them. Sometimes this happens through trial and error, and sometimes through information given to us by a third party. When we are young, we are aware of only the basic lacks: food, water and warmth. As we grow older we learn that certain objects can satisfy these needs, and we learn to feel the lack of those objects instead. Those lacks can drive us just as powerfully as the basic needs themselves, and our brains can operate more efficiently by forgetting some of the relationships between the indirect and basic needs. Gradually over our lives we build up a hierarchy of these lacks. You may be familiar with Maslow's hierarchy of needs, which is based on a similar insight.

Sometimes a person – or company – will set out to deliberately make us feel a certain lack. Think of your favourite chocolate bar. Before you knew it existed, you didn't feel the lack of it – you may have felt hungry sometimes, or even felt a lack of chocolate, but you didn't miss this particular bar. But once the manufacturer advertised it, or encouraged you to try it in a shop, you learned that this product was one you enjoyed, and from time to time you want another one: or, in the language of this theory, you feel a lack of this particular chocolate bar.

Sometimes the lack is placed in your mind consciously and using concrete language, for instance when a magazine tells you that such-and-such model of computer is a good way to get your work done. Then the lack of this computer may be something you become aware of through logical reasoning. Sometimes it is unconscious, as when you wear a jacket, then go outside and still feel cold: the jacket will be marked in your head as 'not very warm' – lacking in its ability to provide warmth.

So in our theory we have people, and they exist in a world, and they have the ability to sense particular wants or lacks in the world. What do they do about it?

The second key part of the theory is **strategies**. People have strategies to fulfil their wants. The strategy may be as simple as 'when hungry: eat food' or a bit more complicated, such as 'when short of money: check balance on credit cards, count the days until I get paid, decide what I can go without or put off until after then, go through address book to see who I can borrow money from', or much more complex than that: 'when feeling a lack of purpose in life: take some time out to think about what makes me happy, read some books, talk to my friends, meditate, consider taking some time out from work, volunteer to help some people, have a beer ...' A strategy like this never really ends, but in order to start it we need to have learned enough about the connection between the lack and the actions we can take in response to it.

A common strategy for satisfying our wants – the strategy mostly studied in economics – is the strategy of buying a product or service. When I'm hungry, my strategy for solving that problem is to consume food, which I am likely to buy from another person rather than growing it myself. If I don't have money to buy food, I pursue a different version of this economic strategy by selling something – usually my time, but possibly my grandfather's gold watch – which gives me money that I can then use to buy food.

Because these buying and selling strategies are so important, our brains have learned a lot of details about how to carry them out. These techniques include processes such as:

- comparing two different objects to see which one is better

- placing a numeric value on things, and comparing those values

- forecasting the feelings we'll get from consuming a product, and determining whether those feelings will satisfy a lack.

Each of these processes takes time and effort, and the more accurate we want the result to be, the more time it takes. Therefore, to get through our lives quickly we take shortcuts and accept approximations.

Of course, we often cannot achieve what we want in a single step. Thus, when we set out to do something, these processes are layered on top of each other many times, or carried out in sequence; our minds construct a series of temporary wants in order to motivate us to get to the next step.

There are a number of specific constraints on our ability to carry out these processes. We can pay attention to only a small number of wants at one time; our brain has the ability to handle multiple wants and strategies in parallel, but the numbers it can manage are small. We can act only on wants we are directly experiencing; any future or potential want can only be addressed by translating it into a current want. And our ability to forecast wants and fit strategies to them is approximate, because the amount of information and complexity involved in accurately understanding and predicting the world is simply too vast to be physically calculable by our finite brains.

These approximations are at the heart of all the psychological effects described in this book. The process of comparing two objects in an approximate way, combined with numeric valuation, governs effects such as extremeness aversion and asymmetric dominance; the forecasting process is affected by priming; anchoring is all about numeric values; and hyperbolic discounting is affected by forecasting.

The details of how these individual techniques are composed to construct the full decision-making process are too complex to discuss in this book, and in any case are the subject of ongoing research. Interested readers are welcome to read my cognitive economics blog, www.knowingandmaking.com, read the working papers at www.inon.com/research or contact me at leigh@inon.com for more details.

Index

99p price points ix, 29, 47–8, 59, 173

absorption 103, 150–61, 164, 166
accessories 154–6
accountancy 7–9, 126–7, 134, 176
alcoholic drinks 5, 8, 67, 95–7, 105, 116, 148, 151–3, 215
anchoring 34, 65–75, 97, 99, 109, 128, 139–40, 148, 152, 164–5, 169, 184, 188, 197, 199, 207, 216
arbitrage 176–8
asymmetric dominance 91–9, 215–6
attention 20, 83, 102, 113, 116, 175–7, 185, 212, 216
availability bias 50

behavioural economics ix–x, 147, 211
belief 49–52, 95, 116, 117
benefits and benefit matrix 6–12, 40, 54, 60, 69, 82–3, 85, 94, 97–8, 105, 107, 111, 124–5, 143, 166, 185, 209–10
bespoke prices 6, 33, 68–70, 110, 157, 188
bowler hat theory; see asymmetric dominance
brand values 10, 45

bundling 120–7, 134, 164, 177, 184, 188, 199, 207
business to business x, 78, 95, 128, 162–9, 176

car leasing 154–6
cash 9, 62, 103, 106–7, 133, 155–6, 197
category; see product categories
cereals 32
charity 179–87
Christmas 63, 176
cocktails; see alcoholic drinks
Coke 81–5, 174
   Diet Coke 59, 148
commodities and commoditisation 25, 68, 83, 121, 149, 153, 199
comparisons and comparibility xiii, 4–15, 32, 43, 47, 58–9, 67–75, 80–7, 93, 97, 99–101, 113, 121, 123–6, 135, 143, 148, 158–61, 169, 175, 194
competition; see competitors
competitive equilibrium 121
competitor comparison chart 85–6
competitors ix, 8, 10, 13, 20, 33, 43, 48, 63, 69, 71, 76–87, 94, 97–9, 104, 124–9, 148–9, 159, 165, 168–9, 174, 186, 190, 192, 200, 206–7

complementary deals 136, 140–1
construal theory; *see* psychological
    distance
consultancy services 8, 33, 51–3,
    68–70, 77–8, 109–11, 157–61,
    177, 199
copywriting 157–61
cost-based pricing 16–22, 59, 62,
    120–1
credit cards 103–4, 108, 125, 214
critical value dimensions 11, 97, 210
customised quotes; *see* bespoke
    prices

day rates 51–3, 157–61, 163
De Beers 166
debts 26, 104
decoys 91–101, 109, 148, 165, 207
    self-decoying 99
    price-level decoys 95–8
defensive pricing 84–5
deferred payments 108,
    165, 184
demand curves 27–34
diamonds 34, 54, 166
diffusion brands 34–6
diminishing marginal utility 96
direct debit 104
discounts 59–60, 71, 76, 111,
    125, 132, 142, 163, 171,
    176–7, 189
drip pricing 169, 194

endowment effect 116–8, 169
energy 62, 89
energy drinks 4, 82
enterprise sales 162–7
estate agent 88, 152–3
ethics 169, 191–3
expected utility 65
experiments; *see* testing

fairness 38, 50–1, 54–5, 124,
    158–9, 168, 192–4, 208

fast food 125, 177
fixed costs 17–22, 127
free offers 79, 125–7, 130–7, 184,
    199, 207
frequency of purchases 3–4, 41, 45,
    147
frequency of responses 37–9
frozen prices 25, 63
furniture 105, 166

giving; *see* charity
Graeber, David 26

habits 4, 7, 56, 60–2, 81, 133, 182,
    208
hairdressing 109, 143–4
Hawthorne effect 164 (fn)
high-margin strategy; *see* premium
    pricing
historical prices 23–26; *see also*
    memory
hotels 45, 128, 151–2
hyperbolic discounting 102–9, 184,
    197, 216

inflation 25–6, 62–4, 188
interviewing customers 37, 41–6

January sales 62–3
jewellery 34–6, 109, 166
just price 50

Kahneman, Daniel ix

law 89, 169, 193–5
law firms 33, 94, 97, 140 (fn), 149
learning effects 147–9; *see also*
    memory
legal services; *see* law firms
line extension 138
line-by-line pricing 126
loss aversion 116, 165
loyalty x, 81, 142, 163, 180; *see also*
    loyalty cards

loyalty cards 130–1
luxury 31, 38, 43, 45, 54, 66–7, 69, 72, 105, 112–5, 135

marginal cost 128–9, 189
margins ix–x, 27, 49, 51, 71, 81, 83–4, 86, 104, 107, 127, 140, 144, 150, 153–5, 169, 186, 197, 200
market research 28–32, 41–3, 44–6, 54
marketing services 157–61
mass-market strategy 20, 36, 83
memory 6, 42, 50, 57–61, 147–9, 175, 212, 214
mobile phones 1, 88, 95, 102, 121–7
money-back guarantee 55, 78–80, 84
moving companies 152–3

name your own price 128–9, 189
negotiating ix–x, 23, 49–51, 61, 109–11, 129, 153, 155, 157–8, 169, 174, 196–8
Netflix 90
Nikon 91–3

Ogilvy, David 41, 45
other people's money 156, 162–7, 193
overheads 19, 21–2

packaging (of services and products) 33, 38, 68–70, 123–4, 152, 198
packaging (physical) 4, 16, 58–9, 80, 118, 171
pain 6–10, 15, 103, 105, 108–11, 163, 165, 209–10
peer effects and pricing; see social marketing
Pepsi 59, 82, 85, 174
positioning x, 1–15, 20, 36, 52, 71, 81–7, 109, 147–8, 184
preferences 135, 142

premium pricing xi, 36, 43, 50, 58, 71, 74–5, 81–4, 86, 98, 103, 110, 138, 172–4
price differentiation xiii, 27–40, 60, 70, 81, 83, 109, 126, 139–40, 142, 146, 149; see also segmentation
price discrimination; see price differentiation
price freezes; see frozen prices
price matching ix, 81, 84, 190
price-level decoys 95–8; see also decoys
Priceline 128
pricing environment 70, 115, 140, 170–8
principal-agent problem; see other people's money
principles of pricing xiii
product categories xi, 32, 33, 43, 45, 76, 80–5, 121, 148–9, 175, 185, 199
product launches 49–55, 58–62, 84, 112–4, 199
promotional offers; see sales promotions
psychological distance 45, 106, 155
publicising price changes 88–90, 168–9
publishing prices; see publicising price changes

questionnaire 209–10; see also interviewing customers
quotation formula 110
quotations; see bespoke prices

Radiohead 128
reciprocity 115, 132
reframing prices xiii, 58–61, 90, 160, 199, 207
refund 56, 78–9; see also money-back guarantee

regulated prices 193–5
relative prices 63–4, 143, 147, 152
removals company 152–3
restricted version 84
retail x, 34, 49, 57, 72, 76, 80–2, 89, 105, 115–6, 125, 133, 140, 150, 168, 171, 175, 177, 199
risk perceived by customers 57, 78, 97, 109, 115–6, 160, 177

sales channels 4, 20, 34, 57, 61, 77, 89, 114, 140, 153, 158, 171–2, 174, 176, 178, 180, 199, 208
sales promotions ix, 42, 50, 56–61, 63, 76–81, 84, 102, 129, 130–7, 153, 186, 189, 193
satisficing 123
segmentation x, 42–6, 54, 98–9, 117, 171, 184–5
self-belief 51–2
signalling 20, 51, 63, 135, 158, 168, 192
social marketing 109, 112–9, 128, 183–4
social media 88, 181
social security numbers 67–8
software x, 6, 62, 85, 126, 143, 152–6, 163–4
Sony 91–3
subjective quality; see subjective value
subjective value 15, 58, 115, 118
subscriptions 88, 90, 99, 102–8, 110, 133, 149, 188, 199
substitutes 81
sunk cost 131, 143

tangibility xiii, 83, 97, 99, 106, 117, 164, 186, 207, 209
tax returns 6, 8, 126
temporary discounts 59–60, 77, 135, 189; see also sales promotions; discounts
Tesco 32, 42
testing 37, 54, 65, 83–4, 139, 141, 147, 207
theatre tickets 128, 148
third party spend; see other people's money
time-benefit graph 107
trials 56, 79, 164, 198

undercutting 8, 125, 169
units of value 10–11, 13–14, 17–19, 21–2, 209
unknown expected utility 65
upselling 136, 138–46, 153, 167, 169, 189, 208; see also drip pricing
urgency 137
utility 96, 211, 212; see also expected utility

value modelling 37
value pricing 24, 110, 150–61
variable costs 17–22, 127
volume of sales 11, 17–20, 27, 43, 71, 83, 104, 106
vouchers 56, 79, 132, 136

willingness-to-pay/WTP 32, 37, 43, 54, 63, 117, 207
wine; see alcoholic drinks